D1590735

Love and Revolutionary Greetings

Love and Revolutionary Greetings

An Ohio Boy in the Spanish Civil War

LAURIE LEVINGER

RESOURCE *Publications* · Eugene, Oregon

LOVE AND REVOLUTIONARY GREETINGS
An Ohio Boy in the Spanish Civil War

Copyright © 2012 Laurie Levinger. All rights reserved. Except for brief quotations in critical publications or reviews, no part of this book may be reproduced in any manner without prior written permission from the publisher. Write: Permissions, Wipf and Stock Publishers, 199 W. 8th Ave., Suite 3, Eugene, OR 97401.

Resource Publications
An Imprint of Wipf and Stock Publishers
199 W. 8th Ave., Suite 3
Eugene, OR 97401
www.wipfandstock.com

ISBN 13: 978-1-61097-780-7
Manufactured in the U.S.A.

All scripture quotations, unless otherwise indicated, are taken from the Holy Bible, New International Version®, NIV®. Copyright ©1973, 1978, 1984 by Biblica, Inc.™ Used by permission of Zondervan. All rights reserved worldwide.

For Sam and Elma
and
For my father

"Each man had to discover his Spain. There were Spains for us all."

—JAY ALLEN, *DEATH IN THE MAKING*

"It gave you a part in something that you could believe in wholly and completely and in which you felt an absolute brotherhood with the others who were engaged in it. It was something that you had never known before but that you had experienced now and you gave such importance to it and the reasons for it that your own death seemed of complete unimportance; only a thing to be avoided because it would interfere with the performance of your duty."

—ERNEST HEMINGWAY, *FOR WHOM THE BELL TOLLS*

"It was in Spain that men learned that one can be right and still be beaten, that force can vanquish spirit, that there are times when courage is not its own reward. It is this, without doubt, which explains why so many men throughout the world regard the Spanish drama as a personal tragedy."

—ALBERT CAMUS, *L'ESPAGNE LIBRE*

"History stopped in 1936."

—GEORGE ORWELL, *LOOKING BACK ON THE SPANISH WAR*

Contents

Acknowledgments

THANKS TO: Joe Levinger, Hannah Levinger, Josh Levinger, Dan Bessie, Josie Yurek, Esther and Miguel in Fuendetodos, Jackie in Barcelona, Gail Malmgreen, Jeanne Houck, Abraham Lincoln Brigade Archives, Sarah Shoemaker, Brandeis University Library, Dale Belman, Alan Entin, Charlotte Houde Quimby, Jo-Anne Unruh, Lianne Moccia, Mindy Schorr, Susan White, Laurie Levin, Alan Warren, Christian Amondson, and Wipf and Stock Publishers.

Foreword

by Staughton Lynd

IT SEEMS that every generation experiences a moment when a course of action is required that may cost one's life.

For activists of the 1960s, it was Mississippi in the summer of 1964. About eight hundred of us went. Three died. In 1936–1937, three thousand volunteers from the United States went to Spain to fight with the International Brigades. Half of them were killed.

Among those who did not come back was Sam Levinger. When he had twice been wounded, the rules of the Brigade required that he return to the United States. Instead he went back to the front. At the battle of Belchite in September 1937 he was assigned a relatively safe task toward the rear. He volunteered to take ammunition to combatants in shallow trenches close to the city who were under heavy enemy fire.

Sam Levinger knew exactly what he was doing. He had written about "the terrific losses of the army which charges into the rifle, and especially the machine gun, fire of entrenched enemies." Nevertheless he proceeded. He was mortally wounded and died in hospital.

It was about such individuals as Sam that Stephen Spender wrote the poem entitled "I Think Continually Of Those Who Were Truly Great," who, he concluded, left "the vivid air signed with their honor."

As Laurie Levinger narrates, when I was six-and-a-half-years old Sam Levinger carried me on his shoulders at an enormous May Day parade in New York City. This was no mean feat. Sam was five feet, seven inches tall, and weighed 150 pounds. I, as his sister Leah gently reminded me before her recent death, was "chunky."

I have another memory of Leah. In the living room of my parents' apartment, she recited Gilbert Keith Chesterton's poem, "Lepanto." Its hero might have been her brother. Don John of Austria, according to Chesterton, becomes aware of "dim drums throbbing in the hills half-heard" and "takes arms from off the wall" to seek combat with a distant foe.

Thus it came about that Sam Levinger not only left (in his words) "thumb prints on the pages of the century" but also became for me the image of what it means to be a person who devotes his life to fundamental social change.

This book presented for Laurie Levinger a formidable editing challenge. She had letters from her uncle, discovered more than half a century after his death in the dramatic circumstances she describes. She found two unpublished manuscripts by Sam Levinger's mother in which Elma tried to imagine her son's experience. She found other small caches, especially Sam's letters to his girlfriend. But Sam was apparently deliberately evasive in some of his descriptions so as to spare his parents anxiety. Laurie fills the gaps brilliantly with memoir material from other Americans who went so Spain, like Alvah Bessie and Steve Nelson. Finally, she writes not only as an historian, but as the niece of an uncle whom she did not know personally, whose memory, together with that of Leah, she sought to honor by scattering Leah's ashes at Sam's gravesite, the location of which she had to discover. There she recited the Jewish prayer for the departed.

Amid the tears that I weep on each rereading of this book, I perceive a political problem that calls for comment. In a letter to "Max," Sam Levinger offers disapproving remarks about an uprising in Barcelona in the midst of civil war. Two things should be said about this, I believe.

First, Sam's approach to other human beings involved in the fighting was consistently that politics should be set aside so as to

further the common project. He particularly honored fellow soldiers who risked their lives, and sometimes died, when trying to
assist a wounded comrade from another political group. Not long
after writing to Max he comments on meeting some "POUM boys,
swell kids."

Second, there remain to this day deep disagreements among
informed observers about the politics of the Spanish Civil War.
At one extreme, commentators like George Orwell and Noam
Chomsky believe that the Soviet Union, as the sole supplier of
arms to the embattled republican government seeking to withstand
massive intervention by Germany and Italy, used its influence to
oppose social revolution in the interest of winning the war. From
this standpoint it appears that the most extraordinary revolution
"from below" of the twentieth century, which took the form of
seizure of factories and farms by workers and peasants, especially
in Catalonia, was permitted to wither on the vine or actually suppressed. At the other extreme, there are those like a high school
friend of mine who has written a book on the subject for German
young people, who consider that the Soviet Union at great risk to
its own security extended solidarity to overseas comrades at a time
when the United States and Great Britain forbade arms shipments
to aid the Loyalists.

I don't think this important historical debate will be furthered
by this book. Rather, Levinger typifies the soldier who through
gritted teeth says to those who write books and articles: "There are
people being killed here, good people, friends of mine. For God's
sake leave the politics till afterward."

Sadly, there was no afterward. The Loyalists were defeated.
One is left to wonder whether the Spanish Civil War, like the
murders of Joe Hill and Rosa Luxemburg, the Holocaust, defeated
uprisings in Hungary and Poland, and so much else about the
twentieth century, signifies a tale of sound and fury without a clear
meaning.

Sam Levinger, I am convinced, would have disagreed. Initially, he felt, it was not volunteers from abroad who saved Madrid. The International Brigades had a critical "moral effect," however. Later, foreigners like himself obviously risked everything side by side with the people of Spain. In spite of all, he wrote, let us "climb the grey hills and charge the guns." Pacifists like myself must climb it with him, even without arms.

Preface

The Story of How We Begin to Remember

M Y FATHER was moving from the home where I'd grown up and I'd offered to help him pack. We spent a long day in the basement, going through boxes of saved memorabilia including stuffed animals and clothes long out of fashion. He wanted me to take a couple of chairs and a desk. As I was leaving he handed me a box, crammed-to-overflowing with papers. "What's in here?" I asked, meaning, I don't need anything else.

"Oh, I don't really know," he said. "Letters from my brother, Sam, when he was in Spain, I think. I haven't ever really gone through them. I think there's a novel, or maybe two—they were never published—that my mother wrote about his life. She got lots of books published, as you know. These two, I never read them either, but I think she probably didn't find a publisher for political reasons. It was the early '40s, you know," as he carried the box out to my car.

It was spring 2001. The next week torrential rains melted the icy, gray slush and flooded his entire basement. All the boxes still there were saturated drowned in the frigid water of an early thaw.

The box with yellowing, brittle paper sat, safe and dry under my bed, saved, but ignored, for the next ten years. After retirement, and writing my first book, I was adrift, without an idea of where to focus next. That's when I finally remembered the box. Reading through it, I discovered a story—many stories, really—of a young man filled with idealistic fervor who left his home to join a volunteer army to fight fascism in a foreign country. And I met his mother, my grandmother Elma, who grieved as her oldest son chose to join the fight in Spain, instead of finishing college and pursuing his political work as a Socialist dedicated to the rights of the working man. He left behind his parents, a younger sister and brother, his girlfriend, and a promising career as a journalist and a poet.

Elma's stories about Sam are from *Death in the Mountains* and *New Hills and Towers*, the unpublished novels my father mentioned. Those novels, along with Sam's stories, poems and letters had been abandoned, saved but unread, in the box for sixty-four years. Reading them left me with many questions that later conversations with my father, Sam's younger brother, helped answer. Still later when I received letters that Sam had written his girlfriend, Clara, I was able to flesh out the story even more. These unpublished letters, poems and stories provide the source material for this book.

In the beginning Sam and Elma share a story, in which they have a conversation with one another, much as they would when they lived in the same house. Later, when Sam writes from Spain, their experiences are rooted in place: Sam in the trenches, Elma at home in Ohio, trying to honor her pledge not to worry. There are layers upon layers of story: Sam's recounting his experiences while trying not to frighten his family; Elma's imagining where he is, what he is thinking and feeling; my piecing together the fragments to create a coherent whole.

Sam and Elma each have a distinct voice and an individual story. Throughout the book, for the sake of clarity, I have indicated who is speaking. Occasionally, there are gaps in their "dialogue" and it is here that there must be a missing letter. Sometimes as I stitched together Sam's and Elma's story, I have taken the liberty of imagining what one or the other of them might have thought or felt. This is not a verbatim history. Rather, it is a story that remains faithful to the essential truths of the times and the relationship between mother and son.

Although Sam was an astute and careful observer, he was also a bit of a shape-shifter, altering his story depending on his audience back home. In one letter it becomes evident that he has tried to hide the reality that he is on the front, and is angry when a friend reveals his whereabouts. And, in fact, there are other gaping holes in his narrative as he travels illegally from the United States to France and into Spain. In his letters from France he plays the part of a world traveler, entertaining with tongue-in-cheek humor. But he never tells his family how he actually crossed the border. To fill in this critical episode I have included first-person accounts from other members of the Lincoln Brigades who climbed over the Pyrenees into Spain.

Towards the end, Elma is left to imagine Sam's experiences, the ones he couldn't write about. She takes the liberty herself, putting words in his mouth, writing in his voice.

Throughout the book, I have made every effort to remain faithful to the essence of Sam and Elma's stories. I am grateful to both of them, each a talented writer and storyteller, each brave in their own way.

I am honored to have met them.

1

November 1936

At Home

ELMA

"**S**AMUEL!" I banged on his door and when he didn't answer I let myself in. I knew I shouldn't check up on him, a young man of nineteen, but somehow I couldn't help myself. He was supposed to be studying for his final examinations that autumn. He didn't budge, and it was obvious that studying wasn't exactly what he was doing. *Why we do this dance about whether he studies or not, I just don't know,* I thought. His sociology book was open on his stomach but as I bent over him to push his hair out of his eyes, I noticed that the funnies from the morning newspaper had been shoved under his pillow.

I pulled out the crumpled sheet. "You're not cheating me, Samuel, only yourself. If you don't want to study for your finals, I can't make you," I said, startling him out of his dreams.

Samuel sat up, grinning at me. "I don't see why you keep worrying about those exams. I don't."

"No, I don't think you worry much about anything, do you?"

He looked away then and opened his book and pretended to concentrate. I went to straighten the clothes crammed into his

1

dresser. Suddenly my hands, busy among the socks and under-shirts and ties, trembled. Because, when I glanced up, I saw the picture Samuel had torn out of the last Sunday's *New York Times* and taped to his mirror. It showed two photographs of Spain in war: one, a group of huddled refugees, the other, several English volunteers in the trenches.

Suddenly, whether he studied or not was the least of my worries.

I turned toward the bed. Sam had closed his book, and was watching me.

"It might be a good thing to go to Spain," he said very quietly.

I tried to drive the panic from my voice. "You're not needed. They've got plenty of soldiers."

"You know they haven't. You've read in the papers same as I did that some places even the women take a club or a pitchfork and go out to meet Franco and the Moors."

"All right, so maybe you're right, but there are plenty of volunteers without you."

"Suppose everybody else would say the same thing? I've got nothing to keep me here, anyhow."

"Samuel!"

"I'm sick of school. The Workers' Alliance here is just about dying on its feet. I want to be doing real work."

"But war isn't work. And you always call yourself a Pacifist."

"No, Mother," he answered gently. "After what I've seen—the strikes, people on the road, desperate, poor, without a place to live, without even enough to eat, and all the rest, I'm a Revolutionist. And today the place for a real Revolutionist is in Spain." Suddenly his eyes twinkled. "You want to go as bad as I do, and you know it. You'd be swell cooking and washing for the soldiers or helping to take care of the kids, when they're driven from their villages."

"I'm too old," I told him. I wasn't fifty yet but at that moment I felt positively ancient.

I said a silent prayer in my heart. Even though I'm a rabbi's wife, I don't pray often. But these were exceptional circumstances. *Please. Please. Maybe they won't send him over because he doesn't have any military experience.* Sam had told Father and me that he regretted that he'd neglected his R.O.T.C. His first quarter at the University he'd registered for the required course, even bought his uniform. But he said he just couldn't wear it while he wasted time learning how to be a tin soldier. Then he signed up for a class in marksmanship hoping he might learn something useful. But the least proficient were weeded out and Sam was the first to be dropped.

His only experience in the use of firearms was on an afternoon years ago. A family friend who had been a crack shot at military school took Sam to the quarry just outside Columbus where he spent an afternoon trying to teach him how to handle a gun. He came back laughing, and declared that Sam might someday become a writer, but he'd never be a soldier . . .

Samuel stood tossing the little kit I had given him from one hand to the other.

"Say, I must have worried you and Father a lot."

"You have. But you've given us a lot of pleasure, too."

"You're not to worry now. I'm so dumb they'll give me an easy job back of the lines. I'll be safer than if I was home—say, on the picket line. You're not to worry."

"I'll try not to. Write as often as you can. And you've got to promise me to let me know if you're sick or wounded. It'll be easier to know than to keep wondering what's happened. Promise?"

"I promise." He stood before the dresser mirror now, combing his wet hair. "Say," suddenly, "should I give a fake name when I get to New York? Would it make trouble for you folks, would you be ashamed, on account of all the lies they're telling about the Republicans, if it got in the papers that I was bumped off?" Before I could answer, he drew himself up as though to answer such critics, "The fascists have asked for it and we're going to give it to them!"

There were a hundred things left to do when the letter came ordering him to report to New York for service with the newly organized Abraham Lincoln Brigade. He dashed into the shower, calling out orders to his girlfriend, Clara, busily packing his clothes, to me, as I filled a mammoth box with lunch for the train. After tying the last knots on the bulky package, I came upstairs to go over Sam's kit. As I put in buttons and a spool of my stoutest thread, I wondered how Penelope felt as she prepared her Ulysses for one of his sudden voyages, just when she thought he was settling down. "But if Clara can't keep him, I can't," I told myself. "I'm only his mother."[1]

---

1. E. Levinger, *Death in the Mountains*, 148.

2

1918–1936

Growing Up

ELMA

Y<small>OU MIGHT</small> be asking, who was Samuel before he became a "Revolutionist"? I can tell you, he was a boy, like other boys. But different, somehow.

It took him so long to walk, we worried that there might be something wrong with him. But once he started he grew so active that Aunt Sally often threatened to tie weights on him to make him sit quiet long enough to eat his meals. First in the little soft shoes I still treasure, later in clumping leather, those restless feet trotted up and down the stairs, out into the yard, down the street to visit the neighbors. Once he followed an organ-grinder, who returned him with a toothy smile and an elaborate apology; several times, before he was six, he ran off to see the world. At first I would search for him frantically; later when I saw how his ripening manhood was shamed by my fears, I forced myself to sit quietly at home, confident that when he was hungry for his supper he would return to me.

Before the Great War, Lee used to say America wouldn't ever get involved; probably just break off diplomatic relations with

Germany. But it started to seem like it would be impossible for the U.S. to stay out of it. What had seemed unimaginable before, now loomed up, a terrifying possibility. The whole terrible mess in Europe had never seemed possible. I don't know, maybe no one knows. Maybe we have to fight so there won't be any more wars.

I talked to Samuel a great deal that autumn about Father and a thing called The War. Father lived behind a glass fenced in with a black frame. Samuel used to lie staring at it from his bed, wondering why Father didn't have any legs.

After Samuel and Leah were bathed and put to bed I always sat down at my typewriter in the corner of the living room. In the slatted white bed, transported from that small city in Kentucky where Lee had his first congregation, to Chicago, the two-year old sometimes woke to hear the tap-tap of the keys. He was to hear them many times in the years in which he grew from a fat, solemn-faced baby into a tousled adolescent. Once he told me that he imagined he heard me typing above the noise of frogs and crickets when he awoke in a barn in the West; he said that another time on a still mountainside when he was feeling rather lonely that he remembered the tap-tap of the keys he heard in his old bedroom at home. I imagine that toward the end, when the spatter of machine gun bullets kept him awake in his dugout, he remembered.

Then the questions started:
"What's a pacifist, Mother?"
"A person who is brave enough not to be dragged into a war. The way your father and I were. Of course, we were lucky and he came home without a scratch. And a taste for French wines just before they shoved Prohibition on us! But I can't help thinking of those who died for nothing. Like your little brother, Moses. The doctor was too busy to look after him when he got sick. The flu was terrible that year and a lot of doctors and nurses were in France, patching up soldiers so they could get well and go out and do more

killing. That baby never had a chance." I could feel the ice that crept into my voice whenever I talked about my dead son. "I don't intend to lose another son in a war."

Samuel looked at me curiously. I know he thought I got too excited over things that never happened. "Is that why you wouldn't let me have that set of soldiers for my birthday?"

"Exactly." I didn't mean to, but I snapped at him.

Once very late at night I came into his room. He woke up and I told him to go to sleep again. We had grown so close lately that he knew I when was unhappy. He sat up in bed.

"What's wrong, Mother?"

I could barely bring myself to tell him. "I kept hoping and hoping, I thought maybe...but they've murdered Saccho and Vanzetti." I sat down on the edge of the bed. My eyes burned. "I didn't think it could happen in America. When you grow up, you'll have to help to change things."

"What things?"

"You ought to be asleep," I said. "Goodnight."

I think he must have stayed awake a long time in the darkness wondering just what I meant.

SAM

And why should we live on a clean street facing the park and wear fresh clothes every day, while if you turned the corner you saw nasty-looking houses with hungry cats among the ash cans and children with dirty noses playing on the steps. One day one of them shouted after me, "Look at the Jew!" The boy's voice wasn't pleasant, and I could tell that he wasn't just passing out a piece of information; for some reason he didn't like Jews. But why? I asked Mother and she explained to me that it was a very glorious thing to be Jewish; but that some foolish people hated Jews on account of a good man called Jesus. Which wasn't such a good explanation, because I was even more puzzled than before.

Religion at home was nice even if it made you keep clean on Saturdays. If you were Jewish you had lots of holidays they didn't keep in school. And good things to eat then that you didn't have the rest of the year like the three-pointed cakes on Purim and a special pudding with orange peel and raisins on Passover made out of the thin matzos you ate all week. Somehow I never got out of the habit of not eating bread during Passover. Once when I was on the picket line, I wrote Mother, what could I do, because they didn't give you much at the Relief Station except bread? But she wrote me back that in war Jewish soldiers are allowed to break their laws and she guessed that strikers were in a sort of war, too. I never knew how much I loved and admired her until I read that letter.

I liked Friday night best of all because it came so often. First Mother would light the tall candles in the silver candlesticks and say a blessing. Then Father read another short blessing at the dinner table. When Father was out of town, as soon as I could read, I would take charge of the blessing. And sometimes just to tease Mother, I'd read extra passages, like the things King Solomon wrote about the Worthy Woman. I told Mother I was doing it to compliment her, but she always told me to cut out the compliments because dinner was getting cold.

Father and Mother always read to us. Father, who said he had wanted to read this particular book all his life, found the story in the library by Mr Hugo called *Ninety-Three* and for days talked about a thing called a Revolution in Paris. Which sounded nice and exciting.

"When I grow up, maybe, I'll be a revolutionist if I have time," I told Mother and Father.[1]

1. E. Levinger, *Death in the Mountains*, 126.

ELMA

Sometimes he would take the long way home through the woods along the Brandywine. Once Father found him sitting in a tree, crooning to himself, quite surprised that the family was worried. "I always get home some time or other, don't I?" he asked indignantly.

We took him to see a doctor who told us that nothing was wrong with Sam except he was restless. He gave us some practical advice: "The boy need adventure, plenty of it . . . I agree with you that you can't let him live in the woods just now and it's not likely that Admiral Byrd wants him. But meanwhile he has to have adventure, plenty of adventure. Take him out to see the world and give him as much freedom as you safely can." Father was able to adjust the family budget to buy a car. When we stopped for lunch by the road on the first lap of that summer's trip, Samuel, after receiving permission to take his sister, Leah and little brother, Joseph, who we called Kiddo, for a "short walk" managed to lose himself in a nearby wood, from which he emerged an hour later with a tastefully arranged bouquet of wild flowers for me. Once in Colorado we heard a yell, and, looking up, saw that he had led his sister and brother up what seemed a sheer stonewall. Now he stood on the very edge of the many-colored rocks, waving triumphantly.

SAM

At the end of our western adventure, we left behind the enchanted wilderness heading back to home and school. I did not record in my journal that on our last morning among the gigantic trees I crept out of the cabin to have a good cry all by myself. Even though I was a big boy now—ten-going-on-eleven—I couldn't help it. Because I was sure I would never be so happy again.

ELMA

In 1931 I won a prize for my book *Grapes of Canaan*. When the $1,000 prize money arrived Father and I decided to take our savings and go on a big trip. I told the children, "Let's do what Benjamin Franklin advised, put our money in our heads instead of the bank." So we took the children out of school for five months and traveled to Egypt, Syria, Palestine and Europe. In Munich, Samuel put on his Boy Scout uniform and went to the Brown House, where he asked but they wouldn't let him meet Hitler.

When he was seventeen he took off on one of his "rambles" and was arrested along with some miners who were picketing for better working conditions. He wrote me on the rough-lined paper he bought from a guard, that he was willing to try anything once— at least for ten days—that the food was plentiful, but monotonous; never mind where he was—I shouldn't worry about him, but I'd better not serve beans when he came home. Oh yes, where he was he got bread and molasses for breakfast, but they were sort of stingy with the molasses, and he knew I wouldn't approve of the coffee.

Neither Sam, confident that he had kept at least part of his promise and written, nor I, who managed to keep going on black coffee and cigarettes, knew that the guards at the county jail kept the pennies prisoners gave them to stamp their letters. But about the time that I was insisting that I could clearly hear Samuel calling, "Mother, are you there?" the way he always shouted up the stairs when he came home from school, a letter managed to find its way to Columbus. Who knows who put a stamp on it, but somehow it reached us the morning after Father had gone to the newspaper to "advertise for Samuel" as he put it grimly. The words, with no hint of the agony behind them, hummed along the wires to newspapers all over the country:

Be on the lookout for Samuel Levinger white seventeen five foot seven hundred fifty dark complexion bushy dark hair brown eyes rough clothing hitch-hiking to Columbus Last heard of in Tennessee September twenty-fifth check transient bureaus jails hospitals Wire collect

Samuel kept talking about writing a story for the newspaper about the coal miners' strike. But that's all he did, talk about it. Finally, Father threatened that if the story wasn't done in a couple of days, he would not take it down to the editor.

Of course, it wasn't easy to start. First Samuel, after I'd reminded him that it was his turn, started to wash the supper dishes. When the dishes were finally done, he simply had to relax over the evening paper. He read through *The Columbus Citizen* conscientiously, even going over the want ads, to postpone the dreaded moment when he would have to sit down at the typewriter. Sure, he knew what he wanted to write, but he just didn't know how to begin. So he'd think the opening paragraphs over first while he ate an apple. And he'd be more comfortable if he kicked off his shoes.

I came into the living room; I spied the apple core and made Sam take it out to the slop pail. He returned with an orange. I ordered him to put on his shoes, knowing he would kick them off again as soon as I left the room . . . Father's step sounded on the porch; he had been giving a lecture some place. It must be getting late. Sam rushed to the typewriter and tapped out a title, just as Father came in and nodded approvingly. Samuel tapped out another sentence. Just then he remembered that he had promised to call his classmates up about the next meeting of the Writers' Club. After that call was over, he sat down again . . . Now the words came so fast he couldn't put them down. The clock struck eleven but when I cleared my throat, Father shook his head and motioned me to go upstairs to bed if I was tired. He had written books himself—though not as many as I had—and he knew that it is unwise to disturb an author when he once gets started. The next morning when Father came down to let in the cat, he found Sam stretched out sleeping on the floor with the finished story beside him.

The Citizen did not pay Sam for the story, but that was all right because he couldn't imagine anybody paying him for anything he wrote. But they printed it, every single word. Sam pretended it wasn't worth saving. But more than once he took the scrapbook out of my desk drawer to read the columns—his own writing!—that looked oh, so much more real in print.[2]

SAM

My story:

Last Sunday night I arrived in Cambridge, the scene of one of the fiercest coal strikes in Ohio. I had heard that members of the National Student League were going to Cambridge to study conditions there. I went down partly to find out about the strike and partly, I guess, for excitement . . . The crowd had pretty well broken up and gone home for lack of speakers when I went outside the county jail with my camera. I called Mrs. Sable, one of the strikers who'd just been arrested, to come to the window of the cell, and when she came I started to focus my camera. Sheriff Gracey, who was sitting on the front porch, came down and reached out a long and muscular arm.

"Hey, boy what are you doin'?"

"Taking a picture of Mrs. Sable and the county jail."

"Well, you can go around and take a picture of the front of the jail. I'll let you do that."

"Sure. But Mrs. Sable isn't around at the front of the jail."

"Either you take a picture of the front of the jail, or you go to the jail."

And since the front of the jail held no interest for me, I went to jail with Mrs. Sable behind me calling, "Goodbye, boy."

2. Ibid., 106.

I was sure Mother would be interested to know where I was so I asked to write a letter, but they didn't let me that night. I asked the chief of police what charge was against me. A pretty serious one, said he. What? Well, it was Communism, or anarchism, or something, and they'd probably send me to reform school.

When would I have my hearing, and would it be possible to get a jury trial? No, no jury trial, and I'd get my hearing in a few days.

"Well," I told one of the prisoners, "I'm game."

"You'd better be," he remarked, spoiling my heroics, "You're here."

I didn't know if anyone had noticed my being taken to jail, and so I didn't know that several of my friends had tried to get in to see me and had been refused. A couple of days later the Sheriff took me out and gave me to my father, who had somehow gotten the letter I sent and had come for me.

I had no charges placed against me, and now I'm out. However, the strikers who have had no charges placed against them are still in, as they have been for over a week. Cambridge today is hardly a place for one who believes in a strict interpretation of the laws of the Land of Liberty.[3]

ELMA

I happened to come into the room the next day when Sam was re-reading his masterpiece for the third time.

"Pretty good, isn't it?" I said.

"Aw, you're just saying that 'cause I wrote it," protested Samuel, always shy before praise.

"All right, call me a liar," I told him, taking the scrapbook and putting it away.

But he knew that I meant what I said; I was a writer myself and Sam realized that if I thought his stuff was good, it was good.

3. Private collection.

As I turned to go I heard him muttering to himself: "By God, I'm going to be a writer."

Although upon Samuel's graduation from high school we had provided him with a steamship ticket, a passport to Europe, and a modest number of travelers' checks, he decided to linger in New York until he could earn his own way. From the refund on the ticket and the checks, he kept out ten dollars "as a stake", sending the rest of the money home with the declaration that he was now old enough to be on his own. The cheapest way to see the world, Sam knew, was to go to sea. For weeks he haunted the docks, roamed from one end of the city to the other, starved blissfully, and filled another notebook with items and color for stories, should he ever find time to write. Once he dashed off a bit of verse which even Leah, his critical sister, liked:

Love's Phrases Vary With The Latitude . . .

In spiced Madrid,
She might have dropped a hot, flame-reddened rose,
And whispered softly from a balcony.

But in New York (East Side),
She giggled from a fire-escape, and dropped
The stiff leaf of an artichoke on me.

He hoped he'd get a ship to Spain some day. Madrid must be a swell place with girls sitting on every balcony and making eyes at you from behind their big, black fans just like in the movies. An old sea dog at the sailors' boarding house to which Sam had drifted told the boy that the wines in Spain weren't so great, but the whores were the finest in the world and gave a man the most for his money. Sam pretended to be impressed.[4]

---

4. Ibid., 126.

SAM

Manchuria and Ethiopia were bad enough, but somehow they seemed so far away. And now this new mess in Spain. Father says he doesn't think those no-good Spanish generals are making all the trouble; he says he supposes that fellows like Hitler and Mussolini want to work through Franco and get their war started that way. I've been trying to write a poem about it, but it's not much good except the refrain: "The fascists are marching on Madrid."[5]

Once when I was hiking I stopped to take a rest; I lay on my back and watched the clouds. They were immensely blue and towered solidly toward tinted billows at the top. They seemed to change gradually and inevitably, piling up and up against the green hills like an army with banners, as the Song of Songs has it. I lay on the grass and occasionally slapped insects. Gradually I realized how calm I was. I was so silent and calm I could have been part of the scenery or the sky. Clouds do not swish or stagger along like people; they simply move. One connects calmness with death, but there was nothing of the sadness, the rockiness of death about this. There was joy in being quiet and watching the clouds marshal grandly. Death seems horrible after an experience like that, though I do not see why I should find simply ceasing horrible. Generally I do not; but I feel ambitious not to pass on until I have left thumb prints on the pages of the century. If only my ability to work were equal to my vague ambitions my parents would now be proud instead of worried.[6]

5. E. Levinger, *New Hills and Towers,* 148.
6. E. Levinger, *Death in the Mountains,* 113.

3

1936

Why Did He Go?

WHY DID Sam go to Spain? What motivated him to join the International Brigade? What was going on in his life, in the United States and in the rest of the world, that compelled him and just a few other Americans to join another country's army to fight a war in which the United States was neutral? Travel to Spain was illegal. Why did they give up the comforts of family, home, hopes for a future, to go to Spain? Were the volunteers all simply idealists and adventurers, seeking excitement? Or was there more to it?

Many of the answers lie in the times, the political idealism and fervor of the 1930's. Sam was born in 1917, so he was twelve-years-old in 1929 when the Great Depression began. Old enough to see and understand that times were very bad. Many, many people were unemployed, desperately poor, barely able to survive; hobos came for a bite to eat at the Levinger's house. His family didn't have much money, but still they were better off than a lot of people. Sam's father, Lee, was the rabbi at Ohio State University and his students often ate at the family dinner table, talking about politics and the union movement. Later, during high school, Sam marched on picket lines to fight for improved working conditions and better wages for workers. By the time he was a freshman in college, he was the veteran of many strikes and an organizer for the campus Young People's Socialist League.

Sam's father had volunteered to serve as a chaplain in France during the World War. Later he described his experiences in his book, *A Jewish Chaplain in France.* He wrote: "This book is a result of the profound conviction that we are forgetting or ignoring the lessons of the World War to Israel, America and humanity. During the war such words as morale, democracy, Americanism, became a sort of cant—so much so that their actual content was forgotten. Now that the war is over and their constant repetition is discontinued, the grave danger exists that we may lose their very influence."

These words and values influenced Sam deeply. He understood that Americans must not forget or ignore the lessons of the World War. The looming threat of fascism and of a Second World War was very real. The Nazi slogan, *Deutschland Ueber Alles,* was a threat to democracy and democratic values everywhere. Progressives knew that Hitler and Mussolini must be stopped, that what happened in Spain could, in fact, happen in the rest of the world.

The Treaty of Versailles established the League of Nations at the end of the World War, that war to end all wars. But, after the war, many people in the United States became isolationists. The treaty included the "collective security clause" which stipulated that member nations would send troops to protect another member country if attacked. Many people were fearful that this would drag the country into another war. The U. S. refused to join the League. Although progressives and many among the Left were deeply worried about fascism, about what was happening in Germany, Ethiopia and Manchuria, the primary focus of the U.S. government was on domestic problems, not international affairs.

But the dire conditions in Spain could not be ignored indefinitely. In July 1936, the volatile situation erupted as insurgent generals, led by Francisco Franco, spearheaded a rebellion to overthrow the democratically elected government of the Spanish

Republic. Most of the officers in the army joined the insurgents, leaving the Republic without a functioning army. Fascist troops were flown from Morocco to Spain, the first major military airlift in world history. By the end of July, German and Italian planes arrived to support the Nationalists—which is what the fascists called themselves, implying that they were the true supporters of the nation of Spain. And in September, Pope Pius XI condemned the Republican government, deploring their "Satanic hate against God". By October, General Franco proclaimed himself Head of State and *Generalisimo*.

In spite of the coup against the democratically elected Spanish. England and France signed the Non-Intervention Pact while the U.S. Congress adopted several Neutrality Acts. Although Germany and Italy were signators as well, in November, in direct violation of the pact, both countries officially recognized the Franco regime. And by late December 1936, the first Italian "volunteers" joined Franco's army.

At the beginning of the rebellion, the Spanish people divided essentially along class lines. The Republicans were primarily workers, farmers, and union members, while the Nationalists were most often members of the upper class, owners of large estates, military officers and the members of the hierarchy of the Catholic Church. This division was a conflict between a new order represented by democracy and the old order that sought to maintain the status quo. The Republicans advocated a more egalitarian distribution of land, and diminishment of the power of the Church and the military. The Nationalists wanted to control ownership of land and maintain Church authority over education.

Constancia de la Mora, a Spanish aristocrat, expressed this succinctly in her autobiography, *In Place of Splendor*.

"On the one side was lined up all the wealth and power of Spain. The big industrialists, the landowners, the powerful Religious orders, the Church hierarchy (but not all the priests), the

Army caste, they stood on one side. And on the other side were the people of Spain."

By November 1936, Americans learned that Madrid was under siege; it appeared that the Nationalists would topple the government and win the war quickly. But, the Spanish people took up arms to defend Madrid. Their rallying cry was that Madrid would be "the tomb of fascism." It was at this critical moment that the International Brigade joined the fight.

At the end of December 1936, a small group of American volunteers sailed to France, planning to sneak into Spain to join the International Brigade. Many of the volunteers were members of the American Communist Party. Sam wasn't, he was an YPSL, a card-carrying member of the Young People's Socialist League, but he was in the minority. Others would soon join these volunteers. Eventually they would number twenty-eight hundred. They named themselves the Abraham Lincoln Brigade.

The International Brigade was an army unique in the history of the world. The Abraham Lincoln Brigade publication, *No Pasarán!*, describes the IB, capturing its essence:

> In 1936 the specter of fascism haunted the world. Mussolini had conquered Ethiopia, Japanese militarism had invaded China and Nazi Germany was rapidly rearming. As the gathering storm clouds darkened the sky, fascism struck another blow. The Spanish army rose in rebellion against the legally elected government. Expecting a rapid victory, they had not reckoned with the people of Spain. Workers, peasants, students and intellectuals rallied to the defense of their Republic...The heroic resistance of the Spanish people gave hope and inspiration to democratic forces all over the world. Madrid glowed like a beacon in the darkness of appeasement and surrender and became the conscience of the world. And from that conscience, a new historic phenomenon was born—the International Brigades.
>
> They came from 53 different countries and there were 40,000 of them. For the first time in history an international crusade of volunteers had assembled to aid an embattled people

in its struggle for freedom. And among them were 3,000 Americans.

Who were they? Why did they come? Black and white, Jew and Gentile, they came from every corner of the U. S. . . . Hitler and Mussolini were the incarnation of everything they hated. Spain gave them the opportunity to come to grips with fascism. They took that challenge and they would stain every major battlefield with their blood. Half of the Lincolns' remain in Spanish soil.[1]

Writers from all over the world were drawn to the Spanish War, as it was called then. Pablo Neruda, the Chilean poet, was among them. While Sam was deciding to go to Spain, in November 1936, the young Neruda was in Madrid, where he witnessed the first members of the International Brigades marching into the city. They were 3,000 strong, mostly German, Italian and Polish veterans of the World War. He described what he saw with his "own eyes . . . even now . . . full of pride."

PABLO NERUDA

The Arrival in Madrid of the International Brigades

One morning in a cold month
In an agonizing month, spotted with mud and smoke
A month that wouldn't get on its knees, a sad
    besieged, unlucky month
When from beyond my wet window panes you could
    hear the jackals
Howling with their rifles and their teeth full of blood
    then
When we didn't have more hope than a dream
    of more gun powder, when we believed by then

1. Osheroff and Susman, *No Pasarán!*, 3.

That the world was full of nothing but devouring
        monsters and furies,
Then, breaking through the frost of that cold
        month in Madrid, in the early morning mist
I saw with my own eyes, with this heart which looks out
I saw the bright ones arrive, the victorious fighters
From that lean, hard, tested rock of a brigade.

It was the troubled time when the women
Carried an emptiness like a terrible burning coal,
And Spanish death, sharper and more bitter
        than other deaths
Filled the fields which until then had been honored by wheat.

Through the streets the beaten blood of men had joined
With water flowing out of the destroyed hearts of houses
The bones of dismembered children, the piercing
Silence of women in mourning, the eyes
Of the defenseless closed forever,
It was like sadness and loss, like a spat-upon garden
        Comrades,
        Then
        I saw you,
        And my eyes even now are full of pride
Because I saw you arriving through the
Morning mist, coming to the pure brow of Spain
        Silent and firm
        Like bells before daybreak
So solemn with blue eyes coming from far, far away
coming from your corners, from your lost homelands,
        from your dreams
Full of burning sweetness and guns
To defend the Spanish city where freedom was trapped
About to fall and be bitten by beasts.

Brothers, from now on
Your purity and your strength, your solemn story
Will be known by child and man, by woman and old one,
May it reach all beings who have no hope, may it
    descend into the mines corroded by sulphuric air,
May it climb the inhuman stairways to the slave
May all the stars, all the wheat stalks of Spain and the world
Write your name and your harsh struggle
And your victory, strong and earthy as a red oak tree.

Because you have given new birth by your sacrifice
To the lost faith, the empty soul, the confidence in the earth
And through your abundance, your nobility, your deaths,
Like through a valley of hard, bloody rocks
Passes an immense river of doves
Made of steel and hope.

Neruda captures the passion, the idealism, and the fervor of
the times. His poem gives voice to the tragedy and drama of the
Spanish war.

It was natural that Sam, from his particular family, raised by
progressive parents, rooted in the values of social justice, understood that the conflict between democracy and world fascism was
the most important fight of his times. It was natural that when
Sam, and others like him, heard the cry of Spain they knew they
must go.

4

January 1937

New York City

SAM

Dᴇᴀʀ Mᴏᴛʜᴇʀ,
    This will be only a note because it's so late and I've a full day tomorrow. Things went splendidly. They gave me a whole suitcase full of woolen junk, from underwear to sheepskin. We leave tomorrow on the *Paris*, the prettiest ship on the ocean in my opinion . . .
    Give my love to each and all. Further details in about 3 weeks from gay *La France.*

R.P.[1]

ELMA

Samuel started to sign his letters with the initials, R.P. I never did know what that stood for, but I could tell that he was trying to protect us as much as he could. Later, we found out that he wasn't always telling us the truth about where he was or what he was doing. Maybe he wasn't exactly lying, more like he was obfuscating or leaving things out, all in an attempt to keep us from worrying.

1. Private collection.

Sam sailed to France on the *SS Paris* on January 16, 1937. Passport # 222217.

There were 101 men on board who were bound for Spain. They pretended to be tourists, which didn't fool anyone. Some of the men with him were:

George Aylaian

Joseph Harold Azar

Thomas Edwin Bennett

Gumersindo Reprisas Bugarin

Jose de las Mercedes Gerardo Bridon y Curbie

Ernesto Rasa Silva Iglesias

John Kline

John Kunz

Oliver Law

Socrates Monastiriotis...

They came from every part of America.[2]

SAM

Dear Mother and Father,

Well, I'm all set for my tour of the continent. I definitely feel, however, that I should spend a little time in Paris at the Sorbonne, especially to perfect my French. And after that—ah, Switzerland, Italy, Germany, Prague, Belgrade, Greece, Estonia, Latvia, Finland, Denmark, and perhaps even Iceland. If only the war were over in Spain I would be crazy to go there. I would be fascinated to see Russia if the Czars were still ruling, but I understand that these Bolsheviks are very different from the Czars.

2. Private collection.

Tell Clara, thanks a hell of a lot for the cablegram. It must have cost her fortunes. Don't do it again. But it certainly was wonderful to hear from you. It is a wonderful feeling, when one is entering into the hardships and dangers of a European journey, with the bath water ice cold, to know . . . but I mustn't get sentimental.

This has been the most luxurious journey I have ever dreamed of. The third-class here is four times as good as the first-class at home. Constance Bennet is traveling first class, and though she tactfully never comes down to third class we often roam around the first-class looking for her, and her very presence on the boat inspires us to our finest efforts. I have learned how to play "Red River Valley" and another good song on the piano.

Seriously, the food is amazing. I am sending you a trial menu. Use it for thirty days and if you do not believe at the end of that time that this is the most delicious menu you have ever encountered, return it, and your money will be carefully refunded. I drink about a liter and a half of wine a day—it makes me easier to get along with.

About the cablegram, I forgot to add that I went around the ship showing it to my closer friends, and everyone felt happy and envied me. It was exactly as if I had just had a baby, with everybody patting me on the back. I hope you don't mind, Clara. They have so few pleasures.

There are some strange people on board. There are some ambulance people going to Spain to do what there I don't know. There are some boys, in fact a pretty good number of them, who are going to France to learn French. They have exercises and Spanish lessons to pass the time away. The chief steward, who belongs to the *Croix de Feu*, says he thinks a couple of them are going to Spain, but I doubt it.

I understand that almost all the crew is Communist or Socialist. The chief steward says that it is *degoutant*. I think so, too.

I have very little to write. I hardly got seasick, though every one else did, and I am very happy indeed. As soon as your business recovers from its temporary financial reverse which followed the crash of 1929, Father, I want you to buy me tickets for the *Paris* by the year, so that I can travel on it all the time. It is the Prince of Wales of ocean liners, the Prince of Wales before he met Mrs. Simpson.

R.P.

Dear Mother,

Been having one swell time in Le Havre. Nothing but pastry, white wine and talking French. I bought a tam which makes me look genuinely French.

Love,

R.P.

Dear Mother,

Carcossone is wonderful. Spent fifteen minutes. Pyrenees etc.

Love,

R.P.[3]

3. Private collection.

5

January 1937

Into Spain

SAM

Dear Mother,
I've been having a splendid time. Everybody around here gives the Front Populaire salute (clenched fist held up to the shoulder) as we pass on our third-class carriage, even the children. We ate lentils today; very good, indeed.

As I informed you this morning we are going into the Spanish Republic tonight. There will be no fighting within hundreds of miles of where we are working; but since the mails are extremely irregular, you may get no letters from me for a long while. The line of work to which many of us have been assigned is rather important, extremely safe and fairly hard. (I can't tell you what it is.) Am sending a couple of cigarette holders; you take one and Clara the other. Also an interesting French trade union manifesto. Please keep it for me.

Plenty of love,
R.P.[1]

1. Private collection.

On The Train

All night long the train puffed though France toward the Spanish border. The carriages were third-class with sharp wooden benches—not comfortable for sleeping. The men slept on each seat packed like sardines. One slept on the floor, and one daring spirit tied himself with belts to each of the overhanging baggage racks. Our first minor casualties were boys who fell off baggage racks onto somebody sleeping below.

Those who lay along the corridors could not sleep—they got stepped on too often. I roamed all night talking to them. The majority were, like myself, going to Spain to join the International Brigades of the Spanish army.

There were Parisian metal workers fresh from their victories in the sit-down strikes; French peasants who hated Fascism because it meant landlords instead of farmers who owned their own land; the owner of a general store in a little French village. There were English seamen, Glasgow textile workers, men who had fought in the Irish Republican army during the Black and Tan wars.

I talked to refugees from fascist countries. Several Germans had just been released from concentration camps; they showed their scars and bruises like medals and were hurrying to join the Thaelman Battalion.

There were Italians, exiles from Italy for a dozen years, who intended to enlist in the Garibaldi Battalion. There were two Estonians who had ridden four days in a tank car, their necks in water, to reach France; a dozen Austrian students, who had skied across the Alps to join us; Poles, Bulgarians, Hungarians, Yugoslavs to replenish the ranks of the crack Dimitroff Battalions.

There were an Albanian, an Ethiopian, two Moors, sons of chiefs, who had been sent to France to study but had enlisted on the side of the Loyalists, though their fathers were with the fascists.

I realized then that I would be taking part in one of the world's most remarkable events, that tens of thousands or so men, not poets and dreamers, but ordinary workers, farmers and students just like me should throw their lives in the scale for a foreign country.

These men who were joining the desperate battle against Fascism were in earnest when they said, "Conquer or die!"

Morning came and everyone leaned out the windows to watch the neat French fields and to salute the gangs of men repairing the railroad. The response was quick and enthusiastic. Up fists in the People's Front salute; up picks and shovels held as we later saw Spanish soldiers hold their rifles.

There was no food until noon; everybody grew rather grouchy. The thoughtful fellows who had filled their canteens with water or wine passed them around for share-and-share alike was already the rule. At noon we stopped at a town and bought sandwiches and wine. The wine was good.

Two of the American boys slipped out of the station gate to buy some hot food and missed the train. When they caught up with us two days later in Spain, they had hair-raising stories to tell about riding freights, astonished French railway officials who had never seen that type of traveling. Once they were in jail, but a group of railway workers got them out and slipped them over the frontier.

Ahead, more and more distinct, grew a white cloud. The Pyrenees! First by train, then by bus we rode deeper into the lovely hills. To each side of us rose the snowy scattered crags, but the pass between them was low, over brown foothills. The few people we passed were darker than the French, and they spoke with an accent which I, with my weak knowledge of the language could not understand. But one language we could understand–the salute of the clenched fist. Salute the People's Front!

Now we were in a little town with both French and Spanish signs. A Spanish border guard, intensely military in his green Catalonian uniform, came into the bus and examined our papers. He had an old fashioned Oviedo rifle with the broad sword bayonet. All the new rifles, we found later, were at the front.

Finding our papers in order, he got out and stood at stiff salute as the bus passed. We had been tense before; perhaps something would be wrong; perhaps we would be turned back! Now that we had overcome that hurdle, there was rejoicing. Two Hungarians kissed each other on the cheeks. An Italian and a Pole tried to dance in the narrow aisle.

A steel worker from Gary, Indiana, grinned happily; then turned serious. "Well, comrade," he told me, "here's one volunteer that's not crossing this border again till Hitler and Mussolini are out of Spain."

My comrade kept his word. We buried him in the Jarama hills."[2]

Sam wrote his family that he and his comrades were able to get into Spain by bus, but most of the volunteers had to climb the Pyrenees Mountains to cross the border. Steve Nelson, the Commissar of the Lincoln Brigade, described that nightlong hike. Already, before the men were even soldiers, they became comrades, looking out for each other.

STEVE NELSON

The guide had been counting noses. He said, "*Vamos! Vamos!*" and I moved toward his voice and found myself first in line behind the guide.

Clouds had covered the moon; we walked through inky darkness, each man following the steps, the heavy breathing, and the occasional muttered oaths of the man in front. We moved through fields, through what appeared to be a vineyard, through another field. A murmuring sound grew louder, until it was recognized as the roar of a stream. A voice called softly, "*Ici! Ici!*" and the guide turned toward the voice. The clouds were thinner

2. Private collection.

or my eyes were growing used to the darkness; I could distinguish vague shapes now. The guide and the man who waited by the riverbank took up a long plank, a two-by-twelve, and thrust it out over the water, and the guide trotted down it. I followed, not happily, teetering gingerly above the racing water.

The end of the plank rested on a rock midway of the stream. A second plank was thrust out from the opposite shore. I achieved the crossing safely. The guide took me by both arms, and pressed down, as if fixing me to the earth—indicating that I was to stay there and wait. At one time a confusion of subdued yells and splashing told of someone's disaster on the improvised bridge. Lewis turned up, dripping wet. "Did you fall in?"

"Slightly. The guy in front of me took a header, and I helped pull him out . . . Boy, I'm in fine shape to start climbing around snow peaks!"

We walked for half an hour, then halted, and the guide went down the line with Lewis as interpreter, speaking to each man separately. We were to keep contact at all times with the man in front. We were not to smoke, or cough, or make any sound. Whenever a halt was made, each man was to be in touch with the man behind him, and let him know when the line started.

Ten minutes later we stopped again, and the guide muttered rapid Spanish to Lewis. Lewis said, "Pass the word back. We're going to go along between a canal and the river canyon. Hug the left. If you fall in the canal, you'll get a ducking, but if you fall off the cliff, you'll be killed. Everybody keep to the left past the sluice!"

I remembered the tale I had heard in prison, of the French youth bound for Spain who fell off a cliff and was drowned in the river below. This must be the place of his death. I dropped willingly to my hands and knees, and

31

proceeded with the utmost caution. Beyond the sluice, the guide waited anxiously. He seemed vastly relieved to have us safely past that spot.

The clouds were breaking rapidly, and the moon shone with deceptive brilliance; it seemed as bright as day, and yet when the line halted, men thirty feet away became invisible, merged with the gray hillside. But at least you could see the ground underfoot. The ground had tilted up sharply; we were really climbing now, climbing into the black wall of the mountains. The ground was soft and wet and clinging. The guide seemed to be leaping from rock to rock, and I tried to copy him, but immediately I missed my footing and sprawled full length in the mud. I seemed to be slipping much more than the others. The trouble, I decided was with my shoes . . .

"My legs are tired. Damn, they really are tired."

"No wonder. We must have been climbing for three, four hours. I used to think I was a pretty good hiker, but man, I'm feeling this."

Lewis said worriedly, "The way those lights look, we haven't come any way at all yet. If we don't get across before daylight, we're sunk."

"Probably we'll make better time later. One thing, we'll get our second wind before long."

We stopped to rest, and a fat little Dutch comrade sank down near me. He was an older man–forty-five. He groaned and panted and uttered tremendous Dutch oaths. "*Foos-foos*," he said. "*Mein Gott, mein foos.*" He stretched his fat little legs before him and shook his fist at his feet.

"His dogs are playing out on him," Lewis muttered. "I wonder if he'll make it." We watched the Dutchman. When the time came to start, he had to struggle to stand up. The effort of rising seemed to take all his strength. Within ten yards, other men began passing him. A tall

Canadian whispered, "We got to go slower. The old boy can't keep up."

Lewis spoke to the guide, and he and Lewis went back to the Dutchman, and I followed them. Lewis said, "Look, comrade. We got to get across before morning. It's one o'clock now . . . only four hours. Must hurry".

The Dutchman looked from Lewis to the guide. "Go 'head," he said. "Go 'head. I try."

The little Dutchman hobbled forward. Despite the cold, his shirt hung open to his waist; you could smell the sweat of his agony two yards off. His eyes were fixed and staring, and his breathing was that of wind-broken horse. He said, "No—no—I cannot," and staggered and fell on his face in the snow. Instantly the guide was beside him, pulling up the frayed wet legs of his trousers. He began rubbing the Dutchman's leg with snow. Lewis copied him, kneading and massaging the man's left leg; and I took the guide's place. The Dutchman's calf was like a rock under my hand, the muscles cramped like that of a drowning man. We rubbed and prodded, and felt the muscles begin to loosen. The Dutchman's breathing improved. He relaxed, and his eyes closed.

The guide was waiting, ready to start. We helped the Dutchman to his feet, watching him anxiously as he swayed, his eyes wandering uncertainly. I said, "Can't we help him along someway." "Not until we're over the ledge. It's too narrow. You'd both fall off the mountain," Lewis translated. "He says it's not far to the next ridge, and there's a road there, and then we can help him."

We tried to explain this to the Dutchman, using all the German that we could muster but we could not tell if he understood. Yet he advanced with the others. Looking along the ledge, we could see the ridge before us. It did not look very near in the moonlight. I said, "Imagine the guy, at his age, tackling a thing like this. I'll bet he never climbed anything in his life before. There's no mountains in Holland. Man, I know how he feels."

As soon as the guide stopped, we turned back to the Dutchman. He stood for a moment, staring straight before him, a numb, bewildered look on his face. His knees buckled. He toppled and fell forward.

"He's through," Lewis said. "He's all caught up. We can't leave him here. What'll we do?" He called to the guide, and the Spaniard knelt beside the Dutch comrade for a moment and then sprang up. He whipped a knife from the sheath on his belt— a Catalonian knife, as long as a bayonet—and with it cut and trimmed a sapling growing nearby, and a second sapling. He laid the two poles side by side and spoke to Lewis. " He wants belts," Lewis said. He's making a stretcher."

Five belts were offered. The guide chose the three strongest and looped them between the poles, at each end and in the center. He worked swiftly, and yet not swiftly enough for his liking; he glanced often toward the eastern sky, scanning the sky for the first streak of dawn. He jerked his long black serape over his head, and threw it over the belts. The stretcher was ready. A sweater came flying out of the darkness and fell at the guide's feet; he grinned and pulled it on. I rubbed the Dutchman's face with snow. He stirred and his eyes opened, and we rolled him onto the stretcher. Lewis and I and a Canadian and a Londoner each took a corner. Feeling himself lifted, the Dutchman groaned and muttered in protest, and tried to sit up. The guide thrust him down, and he lay back weakly, and began to cry. Tears ran down his round cheeks, and he snuffled and groaned and cursed his weakness and pleaded brokenly with the men to put him down, to leave him.

"I no good," he said again and again.

The weight of the stretched pole on my shoulder was less than I expected. I looked up at the sky; it was blue-gray now, and the stars were fading. Below the ridge, on our left, lay a flat expanse of cloud, smooth and solid seeming as a pavement. The guide waited for us and hissed: "Shh! Shh!" he motioned with his left hand: "*Gendarme!*" With his right hand: "Patrol station!"

We went on, placing our feet cautiously, striving to quiet the hoarse rasp of our breathing. The pole cut savagely into my shoulder. A hand touched my arm, pushing me aside. Without a word four fresh bearers took over the stretcher.

The guide called softly, "*Camarades! Adelante! Adelante!*" Faster, faster. His voice was worried, urgent and his anxiety reached out to the group and stung and hurried us. We hastened after him, stumbling. In the east, the sky was perceptibly lighter. The guide pointed: "*Dia!*" He beckoned them on. Faster. Faster . . . Stay down, sun. Stay away from us now. I never prayed against sunrise before, but now I am praying. Stay down. Give us just a little more of darkness, just a little more.

The guide rounded a great boulder, and the path suddenly became a narrow ledge, and a tall Canadian, carrying one corner of the stretcher, cried out suddenly, and disappeared over the bank. The Dutchman clutched the neck of the man on the other side to keep from falling. We thought the Canadian was killed; but in a moment he came scrambling up the ledge, swearing and raking snow out of his neck. But the Dutchman would not be carried any more. He went forward on his own short legs, supported between two other comrades.

It was not possible for us to run, but we ran, and our breathing was like that of hard pressed horses, of running dogs, of the exhaust of a locomotive heard far off—like anything but men breathing. And still the guide danced before us, beckoning us on—faster, faster. He called out something, and Lewis sobbed, "Five hundred - yards - just - five hundred, boys!"

Then we sprinted, the leaden, slow motion sprint of marathon runners nearing the finish, bringing our knees up high as men do, who are leg weary, whose feet are weighted with iron, whose feet can only be lifted by a supreme, scalding effort. The muscles in my thighs danced wildly, uncontrollably, as they had danced for hours: there was a slimy, sour taste in my mouth and throat and lungs were on fire, my blood was roaring in my ears. And yet I, myself, was apart from all this, watching coolly, detached. I saw myself running, my fists clenched, my knees thrown high at each staggering stride. I saw the others running in like manner. Even the Dutchman was running. He had torn himself away from the comrades who supported him, and he was running, his eyes starting from his head. The sky was growing lighter. Lighter. A pale blue, a robin's egg blue, a hateful blue.

The guide had stopped beside a heap of stones. He was dancing around the stones, patting them. He was grinning, shouting something. "*España!*" He was shouting. "Spain! Spain!"

We halted by the pile of stones, and stared down the slope into the valley before us. It looked very like the valley on the other side, the French side, but it was not like that valley because it was Spain. We stared down into Spain, and for a little while the only sound was the snoring, broken gasping of exhausted men.

When we could breathe again, and before any man spoke, a big Welsh miner stepped forward. He had a broken nose and a blood-soaked bandage was wrapped around his ankle when he had cut it on a rock on our journey of the night, and his face and hands carried the blue marks of the coal miner. The Welsh miner said, "Now, lads, this is a good time for a song, and I know a good song for this time."

The miner's clear tenor voice rose sweetly into the morning air over Spain:

Arise, ye prisoners of starvation,

Arise, ye wretched of the earth . . . [3]

3. Nelson, *The Volunteers*, 71.

6

January 1937

Spain

SAM

DEAR MOTHER,
I didn't get a chance to write you until I had been here over a week, because we have been rushing around Spain so fast. Naturally it is impossible for me to name any places, but I can say that I like the country and that they keep me busy. It seems certain that I will never be sent to the front, which does not make me especially happy; but I suppose I am being useful, so that is all right.

Nobody around here considers the possibility of losing. All of them, civilians and military both, say "when we win" instead of "if we win". It is the most amazing demonstration of faith in the armed workers, and especially in the International Brigade that I have ever seen.

I think that during the next few days I may get a chance to do some writing. I've seen a good many interesting things, and if I get a chance to write them up soon they should make quite an epic history.

In spite of the rather primitive conditions and a cold, I've been getting on fine. I actually shaved today. For a while I was taken for a stranger and was questioned severely, but I proved by my passport just who I am. Then everybody admired me very much.

I'm giving a return address, though I'm not certain that your letters will reach me. If not, I'm not worrying. The only thing I care about is that my letters reach you. And at that, I wouldn't advise you to expect any more letters for a couple of weeks, and possibly not then.

Love,

R.P.

Dear Mother,

I mislaid my typewriter so I'm printing. Things are going very well. I'm practically over my cold and my hand, which was a little bumped up, is all fixed. Spring didn't come quite as soon as I thought it would. It gets plenty cold at night. However, the days are very hot so that fixes it up even.

If I had more space and time I'd like to tell you something about the terrific enthusiasm of the International Brigade, with which I have been in contact lately, as well as about the difficulties they contend with. However, about all I have room to say is that I love you all and that you should keep up the good work in the U.S. I am hoping to get your first letter some time soon now. Don't worry if you don't hear from me for a while now, because I've been moving around Spain quite a bit lately.

Love,

R.P.

Dear Father,

It hasn't been a long time since my last letter, but since then I've acquired something I never had before, and I wanted to share the glad tidings. The bunch I work with is fairly isolated from everything. I suppose you get more and better news from the war front than we do, although we see very real evidence of a war here. And speaking of isolations, I haven't gotten any letters yet. I guess when they start coming I'll get a couple a week in a steady stream. Meanwhile, I guess you're all okay.

This is aside from the question. The fact is that we're so isolated that nobody shaves for weeks. I hadn't shaved for 23 weekdays myself, and that's not counting several Sundays when the beard wasn't growing.

A couple of days ago we were visited by a Spanish barber. He had a one ton truck of paraphernalia, anesthetics etc. He shaved his customers on an operating table, shampooed them in the stocks and cut their hair in a crude but effective electric chair. He spoke Spanish excellently.

I was in time for a shave. After I saw the first case shifted from the operating table to a stretcher, I tried to sneak out, but the guards stopped me at the door. I bear no malice. They only were doing their duty.

One couldn't tell by the motion of his arm when he stopped swinging the brush and started swinging the razor. I could feel it for a while though. He worked several hours and then quit for supper. While he was gone, I escaped.

Next day when I washed there was something on my lip which wouldn't go. It was a perfect little mustache! It made a new man of me. None of my old friends will speak to me any more, but I can make new ones every day. I can shave at any time.

Give my love to each and all.

R.P.

ELMA

Many of the men who went to Spain were students, intellectuals and writers, like Sam. Alvah Bessie was among them. He and Sam both described how the Spanish people greeted them when they arrived in Spain. You could almost see the children standing by the tracks, their fists held high in the Popular Front salute; smell the oranges; hear the cheers as the train traveled slowly through small towns.

ALVAH BESSIE

The small towns were relatively close together, and at every one the same performance was repeated. As the train drew into the station the men crowded to the windows, jammed their bodies halfway through the frames. Children and grown-ups rushed down from the town, from the fields, carrying baskets and bags of oranges— large, full, solid oranges . . . The men in the train started to sing, spontaneously . . . and the people on the platform lifted their arms, clenched their fists, stood with their arms raised singing with the men until the train had moved out of the platform into the distance. Little babies in their mothers' arms held their tiny fist aloft, their mothers smiling, looking at them. Our hearts were full, watching them, knowing that they knew who we were and what we were doing there; that we were with them; that we felt their fight was our fight too. They were plain people, working people, peasants and small urban workers, and intelligence shone out of their hard, brown faces, their deep, black eyes.[1]

SAM

On a hill lay a vast stone fortress with grim battered walls, dried-up moat and turrets complete. Near this the bus stopped and we got stiffly out, everybody grabbing a couple of suitcases whether they were his or not. We had reached our first stopping place in Republican Spain.

The castle was rather a grim place. Before the days of planes and artillery it must have been impregnable. It had triple walls a dozen feet thick, a deep moat, now empty, where some goats grazed, and was situated in a splendid position on top of a steep hill.

Its history was grim too. I was told that it was built against the Moors at a time when only a corner of Spain remained under Christian control. In more recent years it was a prison for enemies

1. Bessie, *Men in Battle*, 36.

of the monarchy and the dictatorship. The bravest fighters for Spain's freedom suffered there, making straw baskets in the dim wet cellars. After the Asturian revolt in 1934 those of the miners who survived the slaughter were sent here and imprisoned until the electoral victory of the People's Front in 1936.

The place was very different today. A year ago our comrades had been here as prisoners; now we had come as soldiers in training. We brought our duffel bags and suitcases down to the low roofed cellar and spread our blankets on the boards that were to be our beds. Those suitcases! How hard we worked lugging them around and how soon we lost them! And my mother had packed mine so carefully, too, with all sorts of silly things she was sure I would need at the front!

The Germans, who had been out drilling, marched in singing: "We do not fear the thunder of the cannon! We do not fear the Nazi police!" Then the French, a great many of them, with their rousing song, *Le Jeune Garde:* "We are the young guard. We are the bodyguard of the future" and the British, singing the most ringing of all labor songs:

> We meet today in Freedom's cause,
> And raise our voices high;
> We'll battle here in union strong
> To conquer or to die.

These men marched well. Many of them had seen World War service; most of the rest had served their time in the conscript armies at home. In fact several of them had run away from military service in their own countries to come here. We Americans found that we were the least trained soldiers of the International Brigades, but for all that we proved ourselves with the best at the front.

Supper was good. Beans and rice, excellent black bread and a big swig of powerful white wine. We had rather expected to live on bread dipped in *vino* and this meal was a pleasant surprise.

In the bar room, where we bought the *vino* for about a penny a glass, an American boy cornered me. "Got any smokes?" I hadn't—the French customs officials had seen to that.

"The cigarettes here are one of the horrors of war," he declared. "They call them pillow slips, and they contain two grains of dynamite and one of strychnine each."

He showed me how to smoke them—bite off the ends, lick the cigarette which is too loosely packed, light it, then take a deep breath and see what happens.

One becomes inured even to pillowslips. A month later this same boy was smoking them and "liking it." But that does not prevent the howls of joy whenever a few cartons of American smokes arrive on the scene. Packages from relatives or the Friends of the Lincoln Battalion make many a gloomy day on the front a little less gloomy.

There was an informal show on the wine shop table that evening. I think more and better talent climbed on that creaking table than climbs on the average vaudeville stage in New York. There was a bullfight between two Frenchmen in which the bull took the cloak and sword away from the toreador and the bull fighter had to become a bull. An Irish-American boy sang "Gavin Berry" and the English cheered as loudly as the real Irishmen when he mourned:

> Another martyr for old Ireland.
> Another victim for the crown.
> Whose brutal laws may crush the Irish,
> But cannot put their spirit down.

There I first heard that beautiful song which we Americans soon loved so much:

> On the earth our tanks shall rumble,
> In the sky our planes shall sing;
> With the sun behind our shoulders,
> Songs of battle we will sing.

I had sung it many times myself at union meetings on the picket line in America: it made me feel more at home to hear it.

An Englishman past middle age set the audience crazy with a dance act, half hoofing, half shuffling, and the rest hop-skip-jump. He must have been professional hoofer sometime in his life. I met him six months later in a hospital in Madrid. His arm was in a sling— three machine gun bullets he told me— but he was still doing his act for delighted Spanish wounded.

In the morning we had drill. Right wheel, left oblique, about face. We were awkward but picked up quickly.

In the afternoon we divided into attacking and defending armies. I was in the attacking group which stormed the fort. We took it, but I got a glimpse then of what I saw later in action—the terrific losses of the army which charges into the rifle, and especially the machine gun, fire of entrenched enemies.

That evening we lined up in the square and the commandant gave us a talk, translated by interpreters into several languages. The commandant was a little Austrian, for many years an officer in the Austrian army. He had been on the side of the workers when Dolfus shelled the Karl Marx apartments in Vienna and smashed the Austrian trade unions. Since then he had been a fugitive. He had been in Spain from the beginning and was severely wounded in Casa Del Campo in November. When he recovered he was put in command of this post.

He told us about many things, especially wine. "Spanish wine is very strong" he said. "Drink, but do not get drunk. The International Brigade is no place for drunkards. The first time a man is drunk, he is put in jail. The second time, he is deported. Drunkenness at the front is a court marshal offense."

I nodded. I'd found out I wasn't used to Spanish wine yet and I'd had a whale of a headache when I went to bed the night before. I'd have to behave myself. I'm one of the few Young Socialists who had come over so far. The boys on the boat had kidded me a good deal; I'd almost knocked one of them out who insisted on calling me a Trotskyite spy. I'll show them all I'm not a Trotskyite but a damn good soldier!

Later, only when we were on leave after a long stretch at the front was drunkenness tolerated at all. Even then it was forbidden to fight among ourselves or break windows. On the whole, there is probably no more sober army in the world.

After two days hard drill we left the castle one morning and marched to the railroad station. The village was gathered around to see us off with the six-deep line of children singing "*Jeune Guardia*". It was a scene we soon got to know well, for it was repeated at every town where we stopped. In front, the packed children singing the first stanza enthusiastically, though off-key; the second verse, rather uncertainly with a few arguments between boys in the back row, and the third stanza attempted by only a half dozen sturdy singers. Behind them were massed the older people of the town–a great many pretty girls laughing a great deal; the working men and their wives; a half dozen young men home on leave, or wounded, or exempt from military duty for some physical weakness, and the volunteer militia who patrol the town.

Then there was usually an old woman who picked out one of our boys to give oranges to, and to tell about her son, who was at the front. We understood neither Catalonian nor Spanish, but the fact that these poor old women with none too much themselves, should force fruit on us and refuse payment, always touched us.

After a delay of about an hour, the train started. The last we saw of our town nestling about the castle was a little girl standing by the railroad with fist aloft.

We were traveling through gorgeous country now. Catalonia is the richest part of Spain and the most highly industrialized. On one side was the Mediterranean (I remembered from my child's edition of Homer, how the old Greek poet had called it the wine-dark sea) on the other orange groves stretched back to the snow-capped mountains. Now and then we passed through towns; many of them had factories, sometimes large ones.

In the beach, trenches had been dug; near towns, cannons pointed out over the sea. Fascist cruisers had been prowling the neighborhood and had attempted to land men; but volunteer guards always rushed out to meet them and kept the boats off even where there were no cannon.

Catalonia is at the same time the most militant and (during the first year of the war) the least active section of Loyalist Spain. In Catalonia the workers are well organized, the farmers also; the Anarchists had always been powerful there, and recently the Unified Socialist Party has also become strong. When the military revolt started against the government, the people without arms overwhelmed the army by sheer enthusiasm.

They tore rifles out of the hands of soldiers, they stacked street cars and trucks with sandbags and crashed through machine gun barricades. In all of Catalonia the revolt was crushed with comparative ease. Perhaps it was too easy! Catalonia, a strongly separatist province simply held its own front without giving much aid to the rest of Spain, which was suffering under the fascist attack.

However, in the crucial days of November the Anarchist hero Durruti lead a column to aid Madrid; he was killed in action. Lately Italian bombers have been flying over Barcelona from the Baleric Islands, bombing the workers' quarters without any military objective. Incidents like these have shown Catalonia that she cannot separate her destiny from the rest of Spain. There has been more activity on the Aragon front than ever before. When the great Catalonia army really gets into its stride it will be a tremendous help for the Spanish people.

Barcelona has almost a million inhabitants not counting many thousands of refugees from parts of Spain captured by the fascists; I think most of the million turned out to cheer us. I don't know where they got the energy—recruits for the International Brigades had been marching through the streets ever since those black November days when Franco was announcing he would eat supper in Madrid on a certain night.

In Barcelona, Durruti, the Anarchist leader, was leaving with his column for Madrid. He never returned. The first great wave of workers from every country marched through the streets of Barcelona singing. It was the Spanish people that saved Madrid, not the International Brigades—that General Klever himself has testified—but the moral effect on the Spaniards who had been fighting world Fascism almost alone was vast and telling.

I thought Barcelona a beautiful city although it was winter, flower stalls lined the streets; the men wore flowers in their button-holes, the women in their hair. We marched, I regret to say, very badly. Six men and the sergeant all insisted on giving the step and they couldn't all be right. But the crowds cheered just the same, so everybody was happy.

We marched to Republican headquarters where a man gave a speech in Spanish and the band played. We marched to the headquarters of the United Socialists where a man gave a speech in Spanish. We marched to the headquarters of the C. N. T., the confederation of trade unions, and to the headquarters of the U. G. T., the federation under Marxist leadership.

Then we marched to the barracks and ate a good deal. Marching at our head with a banner was a pretty blond girl, quite young. She was one of the leaders of the J.S.U., the Unified Socialist Youth, which has had such a tremendous growth during the war.

She had fought at Madrid and had been wounded. Now she wanted to go back, but the government had withdrawn all women from the trenches. The reason is rather interesting. At the sight of a dead or wounded woman, particularly a woman hit by an explosive bullet, many of the soldiers lost all sense of danger, charging into blazing machine guns; a soldier without a sense of danger is a poor soldier.

After dinner we marched back to the train for Valencia. The marching was much improved; orders had been issued that only the sergeant should give the step. The ride from Barcelona to Valencia took us till midnight. The scenery was beautiful, the population enthusiastic, the crowded hard seats of the train extremely uncomfortable. As all this was as we had suspected, nobody was surprised or complained.

Valencia, to us is a huge railway station covered by a glass roof, where we ate at midnight. We never got to see the present capital of the Spanish Republic, said to be one of the most beautiful cities in Spain. It was there that we were first formally introduced to the big Spanish yellow pea called *galbonim*, which with rice and lentils has always formed the staple of the Spanish worker's diet. They tasted fine then, with *vino* and bread; later we learned that one dish of yellow peas tastes much like another, and that in time *galbonim* gets monotonous.

Half a dozen young Spaniards got on the train with us. One wore captain's stripes; three were corporals, two privates. They were officials and delegates to one of the youth organizations; they had gotten leave from their battalions in the trenches around Madrid to attend the national conference of the organizations. That's how conferences are held in Spain today–the delegates rush in from the front, there is a furious discussion for a day and a night and the next day with hardly a let up, and then, the work of the conference accomplished, back they rush to the trenches.

Only youth could hold to a schedule like that; it is the youth of Spain, which has supplied the volunteers, the shock troops and much of the leadership.

We started for Albacete, hundreds of miles in the interior, headquarters of the International Brigades. Our leaders suspected that there might be spies and we took turns standing watch over the doors at each end of the trains.

And always there was somebody ready with a wisecrack. Later, during the Sierra campaign the Americans got the name among the International Brigaders of always finding something to laugh at. Where the bombs were falling the thickest one would hear somebody proposing gravely to catch the planes with flypaper, or calling for the end of the round, or something equally crazy.

A good many people considered us rather *loco*; but we never found that it affected our worth as soldiers, and one generally feels better laughing than waiting in tense silence for something to hit him.

Morning showed us quite a different scene from the luxuriant Valencia coast. This was typical central Spain–rough hills, gray and dotted with rocks, with here and there a bright perfectly flat valley pierced by a small stream.

Passing an airfield we saw for the first time the government fighting planes in the air. I had seen plenty of planes at home; but here was nothing like the staid passenger ships. In formations they swooped, dived, climbed at incredible angles, passed over the horizon like a stone from a sling. Some of the happiest moments I have spent in Spain were watching these little things swirl around the sky, fighting off twice their number of pursuit ships and smashing the black Junker bombers on the hillsides. The Spanish newspapers call them *cazas*, which means hunters.

We were a stiff, cramped bunch when we finally got out at Albacete. Peddlers crowded around us to sell us trench lighters and huge knives. The trench lighter, a flint and steel affair, is a wonder invention. The spark lights a bright orange rope, which may be of any length. Some of the Spanish soldiers wear 20 feet of it wrapped around their waists–it adds color to the landscape. If it is a good lighter, one or two flicks sets it glowing ready to light either a cigarette or a fuse bomb. One man in a trench with a stack of fuse bombs and a light can do a lot of good before the attacking force can close with him.

As for the big knives, most of us considered them extra junk, and only the dudes bought them. When we got up to the lines we found that the dudes had been right. The clumsy things were fine for chopping firewood and opening ammunition cases. They were very handy when one was out in the field and wanted a few feet of earth in front to stop the machine gun bullets. Most important, they were splendid weapons for night patrols, where rifles with bayonets are bulky. Many a patrol has gone out at midnight armed only with hand grenades and these knives.

We marched through the streets of Albacete to the barracks, where we ate. Albacete is the headquarters of the International Brigades and the birthplace of Franco.

Dinner finished, we and our bags squeezed into trucks and just as it got dark we swept off to some unknown destination. I do not wish to speak of that truck ride in detail. The crowding was terrific–it was impossible to move a hand without somebody groaning. Then the driver of our truck got lost. He would call out for directions, then precipitately back down steep hills at a high rate of speed, as if full of terror. We knew vaguely that we were going to a training camp, but we had no idea where the front was; I for one was ready at any minute to see rifles sticking through the canvas and to hear curt voices ordering us to climb out.

After dozens of hours some one hailed us in American. The truck jerked to a stop. "Anybody here from Philadelphia?" "Any longshoremen here?" Boys pulled us out of the truck, clapped us on the backs, asked which truck Bill Smith of Brooklyn was on, grabbed our bags and hauled them in. We had arrived at the Lincoln Battalion!

The Battalion commander gathered us in a room and gave a talk. He reminded us that we had had our chance to run back if there were any last-minute qualms.

Now we were members of the Spanish People's Army and must subordinate ourselves to its discipline. What we had been in America did not count—it was what we showed here which would determine who the officers would be. The gravest crimes were desertion under fire, drunkenness in the line, and defiance of the orders of a superior officer.

"We have no idea when we'll leave for the front," he said. "It may be tomorrow or it may be next month. Always be ready to leave at one hour's notice. You'll find the quarters can stand lots of improvement. When we began cleaning up we had to wear rags over our faces. It's better now, but there is plenty of work to be done to make it really livable.

The Irish and Cubans each have a section in our battalion. A lot of them had military experience in the Irish Republican Army and the Cuban patriotic movements. So there's plenty we can learn from them.

We didn't have any mattresses for you boys so I appealed to the mayor of the town. These stone floors are too cold to sleep on. He said if necessary the leaders of the People's Front here would give up their own mattresses, but I don't think that'll be necessary. The mayor will say a few words now."

The mayor opened with the People's Front salute; he greeted us in Spanish. He was a little man with a strong face, as shabbily dressed as anyone in town. He had taken the lead in suppressing the rebellion of the Civil Guard in July. We found out later that he could read and write, being self-educated. (The Loyalists, by the way, in spite of all the fighting are actually setting up schools for the workers and doing a great deal to cut down illiteracy.) Just now he was taking his turn on the city patrol; he carried on his shoulder a rifle which looked like a relic from the Spanish Armada. We cheered him when he had finished.

"There's one thing you know already but which must be absolutely clear," resumed the battalion commander. "We didn't come like O'Duffy's fascists to suppress the Spanish people in the rear–we came to do the will of the Spanish people at the front. The People's Front contains various parties; we are in no way to seem as if we agree with one party more than another. Hitler and Mussolini have sent hundreds of planes, hundreds of thousands of men and a vast quantity of the materials of war to conquer the Spanish people. We are here for only one purpose—to help repel that invasion. What sort of government the Spanish people decide to have is up to them, not to us. For that reason we will wear no sort of party insignia.

"If there are traitors in the rear the Spanish militia will deal with them. Our fighting is to done in one place—on the firing line."

We discovered that this policy was strictly enforced. I heard of a company commander in another battalion who raided a meeting of fascist spies. He was reduced to the ranks because he had raided the meeting himself instead of informing the Spanish militia. By this policy the International Brigades have remained friends with every group in the People's Front from the Republicans to the Anarchists.

After the meeting there was food; I met a couple of boys I had known at home who were willing to talk until morning about what they had done and learned in Spain. However, I was exhausted and sick. Someone had stepped on my face in the truck and the bruise hurt. I found a mattress, threw my blankets of it and collapsed. Most of the other boys did the same. We were to learn that often the worst thing about a battle is the ride getting to it, though I never since have ridden a truck quite so crowded as that first one to Albacete.[2]

2. Private collection.

7

January 1937

Training

SAM DID not write about how they were trained to be soldiers. Maybe he didn't want to frighten his family. In reality, training depended on when volunteers arrived and when they were needed at the front. Some men were at the training camp for a month or two; some for only a couple of days. This was hardly training; it came to be called "five shots into a hill" because on the way to the front the trucks stopped, the men piled out, and were told to fire their rifles into the hillside. Each man got five shots.

In his book *Comrades and Commissars* Cecil Eby describes how utterly unprepared the men were for combat.

> A day or so before the attack, sixty-five new American faces arrived from Albacete, many of them still in street clothes they had worn aboard the *S.S. Paris* . . . Some wore Ked sneakers they had brought from the States. Many were YCL (Young Communist League) members from the Bronx. They had been in Spain just six days and went up to the front immediately. Trucks carried them up from Morata to battalion headquarters, a dugout on a lee slope, where "a tall, lanky man with glasses" (Merriman) welcomed them. From stacks of rifles each recruit picked up a Russian rifle and 150 rounds of ammunition. They were impressed but bewildered—few of these city boys had ever handled firearms of any kind. Before they climbed up to the trenches, a one-week veteran named Robert

Gladnick gave them an hour's crash course in taking a rifle apart, cleaning it, and putting it back together. How to fire it? Don't worry about that now. They would learn that when they climbed the hill and fired a round at distant enemy trenches.[1]

A. Ripps, a young soldier, wrote his father: "The signal is given to go over . . . Our boys go . . . The fire from the fascists seems incessant. Rat, tat, tat, a tat! It goes on for hours. I see another comrade who came across with me on the *S. S. Paris*. His gun was jammed, poor guy was actually crying. I can understand how he feels; like myself, we never saw a rifle before."[2]

1. Eby, *Comrades and Commissars*, 69.
2. Ripps, *Abraham Lincoln Battalion*, 6.

8

February 1937

To The Front: Jarama

ELMA

O NE MORNING as the boys were firing the machine gun on target range, a runner came from the barracks and spoke to their company commander. The Lincolns marched back through the village, carrying the guns on their shoulders to keep them from getting muddy. In two weeks you get pretty careful of the machine gun which you hope will save your life at the front. Instructions were issued at the barracks: "Pack all necessary articles at once! We leave for the front after dinner."

There was considerable difference of opinion as to what articles were necessary. The wisest took only what they could pack in their little knapsacks and a couple of blankets; but some of the boys were loaded down with crammed duffle bags; a few even had suitcases. Sam noticed that it worked out very well: those who carried the most lost it the soonest.

Again the whole town was out to see the men off. There was a great deal of enthusiasm and confusion, with women crying, and men giving the Lincolns raisins and oranges, and the children singing different songs—all at the same time. One by one the trucks roared off the highway. A little white dog raced after the truck on which Sam rode until the driver heeded his pleading to "stop and take the cute little devil in." An Albanian boy from Connecticut who always amused his comrades with his quaint English adopted the little fellow and fed him on canned beef. But at the first artillery bombardment at the front, the dog became panicky and ran yelping down the road never to return. The Albanian said regretfully that the pup was not cut out to be a soldier.

They rode steadily until the middle of the next afternoon; they had turned off the main Madrid-Valencia highway and now traveled south. The hills on both sides of the valley became higher, more barren and savage, although the valley itself was pretty with fruit trees just beginning to bloom. Sam thought of the hills back home looking over the Ohio River. Several times ambulances hurrying from the front rushed past.

The Lincolns had just got out to eat at the little town of Morata, when someone heard an airplane droning. The boys behaved well, considering this was the first time they knew the terror from the skies: they spread out as ordered, lay under trucks and in ditches.

When the bombers had definitely gone, the Lincolns assembled and group leaders were appointed and assigned their groups. The commander of Sam's machine gun company spoke briefly: "We're going up to Jarama," he said. "The enemy has been making a terrific drive to break through and cut the Madrid-Valencia road. You all know what that would mean—starvation for Madrid. The enemy has had a great advantage so far both in numbers and equipment; but we have the positions and there is no reason why we shouldn't continue to have them. The Lincoln Battalion is now going into reserve position until orders come to move into the front line."

When evening came they moved up toward their position. There were no lights except when the leading truck flashed a signal. An Irish boy, sitting beside Sam confessed: "I worry all the time except when I'm singing." He broke into the latest jazz.

The trucks climbed for a while, then stopped; the men got out. They grouped by the side of the road; some carried the packs of the gunner and second gunner who would have to pull the gun. That first night dozens of useless articles ranging from books to pajamas were thrown away by men who had grown tired of carrying them.

As he stumbled up the dark hill Sam for the first time heard the wail of a spent bullet and the plop as it hit the ground. It gave him a thrill then; before a week had passed he forgot to notice such trifles. Like his companions it did not take him long to learn to ignore bullets which had passed—there were plenty of bullets ahead to take cover from. "Close only counts in pitching horseshoes," became a good phrase to shut off anyone who began detailing what a narrow escape he had had.

Sam's machine gun group became separated from the rest of the company. There was no use trying to find anyone in the dark; the men rolled themselves in their blankets, as the night had grown chilly, stretched out in a ditch and went to sleep. Tired as he was, Sam had a hard time falling to sleep. The bullets squealed overhead or kicked the ground; once in a while he could hear a shell exploding a long ways off. He wondered whose it was—it must be a fascist shell he decided for the Republicans have very little artillery on this front. He wondered whether it had killed anybody. He was learning that it took a little while to get used to a war.[1]

ALVAH BESSIE

In these vineyards and in the pinewoods on the hills beyond, we were beginning to learn the trade of the soldier. It is a hard trade, and one that does things to you as a man; that changes you from one sort of man into another. It is not easy to be a good soldier, and for a middle-class intellectual who had spent most of his conscious life in the sedentary pursuit of finding words for things he believed he felt, it was an almost impossible life.[2]

Elma must have wondered what sort of man Sam was turning into. Who would he be when he came home?

1. E. Levinger, *Death in the Mountains*, 165.
2. Bessie, *Men in Battle*, 53.

9

February–May 1937

Letters home

S AM KEPT his promise and wrote many letters, often including stories and poems. He wrote to Clara saying how much he missed her; he wrote his friend Max about the political situation in Spain. He promised he'd try to find time to write an article for *The Nation*.

SAM

Dear Clara,

I'm expecting a letter from you any month now. Letters take a long time from here to there, but I probably won't move till a month or two, and so the address I give at the bottom is correct, I think. I'd like to hear from you.

Tell everybody things are wonderful and grand. In the words of Ernest Thompson Seton, spring is coming. We went out for a walk a few days ago. Two big trucks which were supposed to take us to a bullfight at a town ten miles away didn't show up. We waited till three-thirty in the afternoon and then a dozen of us started walking on a big scale. The little white flowers were just coming out in big droves, and the hills were all beautiful. This is in its own way one of the prettiest countries I've ever been to, especially in the spring.

About eight miles down the road we met the trucks, going the other way. The drivers had stopped to see the bullfight themselves. They reported that the matadors had won every encounter, without exception. In the last everybody thought the bull was dead, and they were swarming onto the field when the bull got up and swarmed them off again. So the bull won a moral victory, although the matador revenged himself by cutting off the leg and throwing it to the mayor.

I'm going to write an article, maybe, and send it to the editor of *The Nation*. I'll ask him to send it on to you or mother if he can't use it. Tell Mother if she thinks it is any good to send it to a couple of places. I'd like to use my name on it, naturally, but I don't know conditions in the States well enough to be sure whether that would be safe, so that must be up to you. And at that I may never write the article, so don't wait too anxiously.

I don't get sentimental by mail as a general thing, but I just wanted to say that since I left I have met just as nice people as you and didn't like them nearly as well. This may be clumsily phrased, but it is meant as a compliment. I seem to love you a great deal.

Hope you're having a swell time—and getting good grades.

The paper tore, so I think I will quit writing now. There's very little to say anyway except that this is a wonderful country, that some extremely good work is being done here, and that it would give me a great deal of pleasure to be with you again. That may possibly be accomplished within the next year or so.

Give love to all the Levingers.
Socoro Rojo, Rm. 17.1
Albecete, Spain

Sam's article was published in *The Nation* on May 8, 1937, using the initials, R. P., his *nom de guerre*.

SAM

With the International Brigade by R.P.

In the first place, I can't give any news. The boys here often wish that they could get a copy of *The New York Times* or *The Daily Worker*. Then they could get some news, even inaccurate. I don't think anyone knows less about what's happening in a war than the soldier in it. If we see a fascist bomber crash in front of us we know about it: if it crashed over the hill we either hear nothing about it, or we hear that the rebels attacked, but were beaten back with terrific losses, and one of their tanks exploded. So I'll only tell you what I saw, and what men from the front told me, and my own impressions.

Speaking of airplanes crashing, there's nothing more exciting than lying on the ground and watching a really good dogfight in the air. On our way here we went through a good bombing. We had gotten out to eat at a little town when someone heard an airplane droning. Approaching us, low on the horizon, were three big dots, marshaled by tiny specks. In half a minute they were three distant monoplanes, German bombers, surrounded by pursuit ships. In another thirty seconds they were the most terrifying things I have ever seen, three low black immense bombers directly overhead, dropping white packages which looked neat like ants' eggs. Curiously enough, every damn one of those packages was falling directly at me.

The mothers were herding their little children into doorways. Really, a man can be cut just as deeply by flying metal as a child can; but these children with silky hair looked so defenseless and soft that I thought more of them than of myself. I never felt so deep a sense of tragedy as when, a few minutes later, I was digging and pulling around debris and recognized a little girl I had seen playing around.

There were three of us in the ditch, one in front of me and one behind. They started discussing the war situation, with a local emphasis. "Look, they're dropping leaflets!" yelled one of them. He was a good soldier, but this was his first airplane raid. "Hell!" said the other, "they look like bombs to me." Just then there was an earthquake and the trench started spinning like a roulette wheel. That was the first bomb. About the time I had cleared my head the next one dropped. If the first had been close, the next was almost on top of us. This gave rise to the thought: where would the third one be? It was close enough to send bricks whizzing about over heads, and our ears rang for hours, but still it missed us.

Suddenly there was a drone from another direction, and tiny planes with red wings flashed from a great blue cloud like lightening. There was a rattling like the little whirring noise-makers children use on Halloween. The sky was terrifically confused. Little red planes were climbing, swooping, following little white planes or being followed by them. The rattle increased and decreased and increased again.

The last two of the three bombers turned around with a sweep and started back. What happened to them I don't know. As they turned they dropped their bombs, all at once, but they were rushed and missed the town. One of them destroyed an olive grove, while the other prepared a dry hillside for cultivation. The first bomber dove down the valley at a terrible speed with a red-winged pursuit plane clinging behind it. I turned away for a second to watch the fighters about me stitching the sky, and when I turned back there was only a cloud of smoke from a hillside.

Then came the job of pulling wrecked houses to pieces to find the bodies, crushed or hacked out of shape but still alive. I won't go into that. The bombs had not injured any of the soldiers in town, but they had done a good deal of damage near the market. I saw over a dozen civilians, chiefly children, carried away from a house where they had gathered. The United Socialist Youth (J.S.U.) is pushing plans to "make each village a fort" by having shock brigades build bombproof dugouts.

I meant to spend less time on the air-raid and more on the state of the nation. What impresses one immediately is the complete, unbroken solidarity of all the workers and peasants in wanting the war won and the whole former state of affairs overturned. If one happens to whistle the "Internationale" while going down the street two or three people going the other way will start singing it on the spot, and one can hear their voices going into the distance. The children are loaded with badges and with pictures of Largo Caballero, La Pasionaria, and Pablo Iglesias, and will give the People's Front salute (clenched fist to shoulder) at the slightest provocation. For that matter the greeting used by everyone is "*Salud!*" with the clenched fist. I went to the fountain yesterday to get a drink. There was an old woman with a great pottery jug there before me but when she saw my International Brigade badge she wouldn't consider finishing filling her jug before I had drunk. They catch us and read us letters (in Spanish, an unknown language) from their sons at the front, dose us with oranges, bread and too much *vino tinto*, and when they turn us loose, ask us to look up their brothers in Montevideo, Uruguay, when we return home. (Their conception of the western Hemisphere is hazy.) In fact, they were even more cordial to us than to their own boys, for we have come from a distant, almost mythical country to fight against the fascists and the landlords and the foreigners who send the bombing planes over their houses.

And we seem to be beating them. From everything I have seen we are forcing them back step by desperate step. Nobody anymore considers the chance of their taking Madrid. A cockney expressed it to me like this: "So General Mola had to stop the advance on Madrid. For why? 'Cause he had to wait for his white horse, so he could ride into Madrid in style. But while he was waiting the Internationals come in, and the Anarchists from Barcelona and the Socialists from Asturias and the Communists from Guaderama, and Mola's white horse turned out to be a bleedin' white elephant. So if he ever rides into Madrid now it'll be on a white donkey with his hands tied behind his back."

News has been coming from Guadalajara which might mean that the war will be pretty short. But long or short there seems little doubt about whose victory it will be.

Mobilize every possible group to give aid to Spain. Material aid is needed—the non-intervention committee has given us plenty of moral aid. The Spaniards treat the non-intervention committee with respect but suspicion. A friend of mine going to the front told me: "I've got a little rifle here. Now I'm just an average shot, but I put more faith in that rifle than I do in every damn non-intervention pact between here and Tahiti."

So get the boys busy mobilizing help and sentiment, and make any use you can of this. I feel convinced that this fight in Spain is extremely important for the future of the world. Those of us whose future is going to be connected with that of the world for any length of time should consider that it's important to our future as well.[1]

1. S. Levinger, "With the International Brigade."

10

February–April 1937

Stories from the Trenches

SAM

They Were So Peaceful

THE LINCOLN Battalion sat in its Jarama trenches, eating breakfast and criticizing the coffee. "It'd make good tea," said the corporal. I announced that it tasted like grapefruit juice.

Two hundred yards away one of our fascist neighbors was taking his finger exercises. Up and down the side of the trench. The explosive bullet makes a nasty noise; it makes a nasty wound, too. But the boys hardly noticed the shooting until a bullet skimmed the top of the trench, scattering sand in the coffee. Harry grabbed his rifle and glared at the fascist trenches through a peephole.

"I'll kill any sniper who ruins my coffee!" he growled, while the boys laughed.

"You can kill him after breakfast if he's not a better shot than you are," answered the corporal genially. He turned to me: "How long's it been since you took a bath?"

"I don't know, a while." I was preoccupied at that moment wondering what I should print for a new sign for my dugout. I was very proud of that dugout and insisted that I entertained fewer

64

fleas than any corner of the trench. I was particularly fond of the notice I had put over the rudimentary bar: **Yes, We Serve Lobsters! Sit Down!**

"What did you say?"

"I said how long was it since you had a bath?"

"Oh, months, I guess," I told him, since I couldn't remember the last time.

"You can go down to Morata today to bathe. And while you're at it, a bunch of boys are going to look over the cemetery there to see how it's kept and so on. If you want to, you can go for your own group."

So I and the others who were to go down walked through the communication trenches into the grove of bullet-hacked olive trees, and down the grey rocky hill. And now and then a stray bullet whined by, hissing, pleading, whispering its desire for blood. But by this time we'd learned not to worry too much about stray bullets—you don't hear them in time to duck, anyway–and we walked down the dusty road, watching the little lizards run between the yellow flowers and grey scrub.

It was good to have a bath again. The slim boys joyfully covered themselves with lather; washed it off; then bawled for more soap. Throw the old clothes in a pile—they'll boil the lice out of them–try to get new clothes to fit. Those pants are just a few inches big; a belt'll keep 'em up. You lost your belt? O. K. O. K. Here's another pair. Too small? Hell, you're never satisfied!

Finally the baths were finished, or better phrased, we were ejected to make room for the next group. We wandered through the shell-battered streets of Morata (we called it Neuritis, just as we called the next town, Perales, Paralysis), passed the guards at the edge of the town by explaining our mission in broken Spanish, and reached the great iron gates of the little cemetery.

How Mother would enjoy this, I thought. She always was such a great one for visiting cemeteries. Sleepy Hollow when we were kids and made that eastern trip; that place where Helen Hunt or somebody was supposed to be buried in Colorado. Teased Mother by asking whether they were related. Gray's Country Churchyard in England; Disraeli's grave the next day; he was a dandy like Eden, but must have had more brains. Shakespeare's tomb, of course. Ghoulish taste, I called it. But she seemed to enjoy it. Have to write her about this.

The gates creaked and struggled. The middle of the plot was taken up by big white family tombstones. There were solid squares of marble and towering obelisks, and there was one family vault with a long list of *Dons* on it. This is the only place you landlords are going to rule from now on, *Señors Dons!* I told the dead. But our dead did not lie under long white tombstones.

In a long common grave, under a plaque made from the back of an ammunition box, lay the dead of the Dimitrov Battalion. Someone had twisted a little wreath of daisies and dropped it over the grave. For the present, a daisy chain is all these gallant comrades need. A free Spain, a liberated world, will someday be their monument.

These were the men who went up to Jarama to meet the German and Italian shock troops. With the Dimitrov Battalion as the spearhead, the Republican Army, outnumbered three to one, smashed the Reichswehr regulars. They had no planes to bring down the furious bombers, no artillery support, not one tank. Yet they stopped the fascists; the Madrid-Valencia road was saved and Madrid still fed and armed.

But I would like to know who left the daisies there. It might have been a soldier. We had a comrade—he is dead only a few days—who used to decorate the graves wherever he found them. Or it might have been a child from Morata for the children worshipped the International Brigades, following the volunteers through the streets and singing to them. Or perhaps one of the girls of Morata remembered a Dimitrov boy, for men facing death make earnest lovers.

There were no Americans there. Gravely my comrades and I gave the salute to the dead—the clench fist lowered. Then we went slowly out, shutting the creaking gates.

A mile from the line, a dead bullet plopped near the us. One of the boys started whistling the famous fighting song of the German workers. He had learned it from a comrade in the Dimitrovs:

> There stands a man, a man, strong as an oak;
> He has already been through many battles.
> Perhaps he will be a corpse before morning,
> As so many fighters for freedom are.

We sang it in the German in time with the step. Left–left–left foot in time with your comrade's left. It was not depressing to see that grave; rather, as we sang there was a thrill of pride. We were the vanguard of life; we who loved life so much had volunteered to risk death to stop Fascism and to help a sane world be born.

I tried hard to forget Big Jim, shot through the guts, a twisted heap of foul rags, not the kid, who laughed and sang and had a girl back home and meant to get married after the fascists had been kicked out of Spain. Big Jim! And all the others! Even some of those kids on the other side! Italians thinking they were sent to fight in Ethiopia; Spanish peasants, conscripted into Franco's armies, or inflamed by lies of desecrated churches and ravished nuns. Twisted heaps of foul rags. I'm a crack machine gunner now, the corporeal says. I've killed my men, too. Why do we have to do it? If we ever get back home–baths and no bombings and sticking your head out when you feel like it—will our hands ever feel clean? Or are those fellows back there the only ones who can really forget?

The Dimitrov dead were so peaceful.

A Rifle Called Mary

Jim yawned; then with a twist of his body rolled to his feet. From his shoulder hung his rifle with "Mary" carved in bold white letters across the butt. Rifle swinging from his shoulder, neck strong and head erect, Jim strode adventurously into the trench.

There was no moon, only a glimmer of starlight. My eyes searched between the grape vines, found nothing. Jim used to say that I was the best guard on the line because I was always scared to death.

I was thinking of the big drive to start next day. I was wondering if I would be killed, or wounded, or whether I would go unhurt, and my speculations gave me no answer, for it is only chance connection with a hurrying piece of lead that decides whether a young man will live forty years or forty seconds. At least I hoped I would not get wounded by an explosive bullet—I had seen the crude raw gaps they made.

Jim walked down the trench, limping just a shade. He had come back from the hospital the day before without any papers certifying he was cured. At first he claimed he had lost them, but afterwards he admitted he had run away from the hospital. Since he was here there wasn't much to be done about it; he was bawled out and given his old job of section leader.

"How's the wounded hero?" I asked him.

"Just fine. How's your dead head? Feel any signs of life in it lately?" he countered, grinning.

"How did you come to get hit anyway?" I asked. "You went down the road to get water and then the airplanes started spilling bombs, and that's the last we saw of you."

Jim sat on a firing step. "I was walking down the road from the town where I'd taken a drink out of the well at the crossroads. That had been half an hour ago, and since I felt OK, I was pretty sure the fascists hadn't poisoned the water. So I started back with twenty-some canteens strung over my shoulders. I looked like a fish in a net.

"I was keeping a good look-out for aviation. You remember, they bombed the town once that morning, but without much luck. I figured they might try again—if they could stop men and supplies from coming along that road, they would probably delay the advance.

"I was thinking about Mary, too. I'd gotten a letter from her the morning before. Doing fine as usual. There's lots of things happening in America and she's taking her part.

"I saw the planes come over the horizon, but I thought they were probably ours. I kept on walking, staring at them. More planes came suddenly from another direction, too: I noticed them when I heard the anti-aircraft guns complaining, and saw the white powder puffs dotting the sky.

"From two sides the planes swept down on the trembling town. There was blasting in a field to the right of me; the dirt shot up and then thick smoke rose. An anti-aircraft shell burst right in the middle of a squadron. One of the planes tipped curiously and then headed back toward the fascist lines with white smoke streaming behind. That was the first successful anti-aircraft I had seen; I think I cheered a couple of times as I lay in the wide shallow ditch, but about that time I quit cheering and began gulping because the three black Junkers were dropping their white bombs.

"When you see those bombs falling, you don't feel fear so much as dismay, despair. I lay still and gripped the grass roots with my fingers. The knowledge of death was on me; I felt it even plainer that I had felt it the day before, when the snipers were searching for a hole in the machine gun plate. There was a terrific shock next to me, and then a second later another still worse. I was biting my lip and I guess I must have drooled a little, too, because my chin was wet. Then something smashed all around me, not just in a particular direction, and I heard the rocks going up in the air. The first one that hit me was on the place I generally sit down, and I said out loud: 'Ooh, a direct hit with a bomb!' Then another one hit me in the back, and I just 'ooh-ed' and quit talking because I was out like a light.

"When I came to I was gasping like a fish in a gas attack. I couldn't seem to get any air in. I forgot to exhale, just tried to crowd more and more into my lungs so I could breathe. But no go.

"I looked up, and there were the planes going around my head like a halo. I'm pretty cool mostly, and I realize that planes aren't in a class with the machine gun for the number of soldiers they kill, but, Goddamn, I was seized by panic. The bombs were falling way off now—they were trying for the town and damn well couldn't hit it. But I think that what broke my nerve was that I couldn't get up, nor hardly move, just lay there and gasp.

"Finally the planes went home and I toppled to my feet. Boy, there were hunks of shrapnel lying all over the neighborhood, right up to a yard from me. The bank had saved me from them–they'd have run through me like butter.

"That steadied me up. If they had that good a chance at me and couldn't get me, there wasn't much to worry about. I started along the road into town; but I made a gloomy job of it. I felt like I'd been ripped open and spilled over the road. All the same I knew it wasn't so serious, just a couple of bad bruises.

"I got to the place they used as a hospital. Up to the day before it had been the headquarters of the fascists and also a phony union modeled on Hitler's Labor Front. All around the place lay posters and cards and propaganda of all kinds. The doctors couldn't spare much time for me when they saw I wasn't wounded. The bleeding were coming in in a stream, including fascist prisoners. They set me in a chair and I crumpled down on the floor, with my face on a poster showing an inspiring young officer painting out all the initials which stood for unions and political parties, and painting on a bunch of arrows representing the fascists.

"War's a pretty terrible thing. They brought in a kid, a *rubio*—you know, that's what the Spanish call blonds. His waist and belly were as soft and slim as a girl's—but his upper leg, although it was still there, was just waiting to be clipped off. God, the poor kid yelled.

"All the time I was still nervous and shaky. There's plenty of things in a war that sound like planes and bombs. Every time a car door slammed or a shell burst, I'd shiver and cling to the cracks in the floor. Finally two tired First Aid men supported me over to the ambulance and shuttled me on a stretcher."

Jim was silent. "Some ride," I said.

"It was long and it hurt. There was a Frenchman with two fingers shot off and he swore like Hell when we jolted. Under me there was a guy shot some place in the body—the spine, I imagine; he was only partly conscious, and kept hiccupping with a peculiar note that had a little scream in it. I groaned every time it bumped, chiefly to give vent to my feelings.

"There was a good hospital at Madrid; swell nurses and the best food in Spain. The nurses really are honeys. For one thing, they're always working. They start at six in the morning, and if you go to sleep at midnight, they're still blustering around. Blustering is the word–they rush around turning over mattresses, intimidating everybody, and saying, '*Tu mucho pinto!*' As near as I can figure it out, that means, 'So you're a wise guy, eh?' Another thing, a girl must have to win a beauty contest to be a nurse in Spain."

"You speak wistfully," I remarked. "You talk as though deep personal experience had influenced your judgment."

"It might have at that," sighed Jim. "She was goddamn pretty and we had a good time together for a couple of days. Just a little fooling around. It only made me realize how hungry I am for Mary. Hell, why don't this war quit so I can go home to my *novia*?"

"But what was the idea of leaving the hospital before you were cured?" I asked.

"I heard the big drive would be on in a couple of days and I wanted to be with the battalion. I knew I was well enough to hold up my end. The fascists were shelling Madrid pretty heavily the last couple of days I was there. There were a good many planes up, too, but ours brought them down in a hurry. I saw some damn good air fights. But when I'd hear a shell pop—you can hear them a long ways, you know—I'd think, 'Now what the hell is a volunteer for liberty doing here, living luxuriously in a hospital when he should be out fighting?' I'm no hero or anything fancy, but it got so my one aim in life was to run those bastards out of shelling range of Madrid. And I said I was going out for a drink of orangeade, and here I am."

There was a long pause. Jim was musing. I strained my eyes into the darkness, but said nothing. "How do you think we'll come out of the drive tomorrow?" I asked. I had a good deal of respect for the way Jim sized up situations.

"On top. Those that are left will, anyway. We'll smash them this time; but it'll cost plenty of lives to do it. I'm glad we're starting it though. If I live, I'll be back with Mary in a couple of months. If I don't . . . But I wish to God I hadn't been made section leader. It's more responsibility for the lives of men than I like. I wish I still was a number one gunner on a Maxim."

He started up. "I'd better be on my way, kid. We'll have full day tomorrow. And, kid, if I should get nipped try to get hold of my rifle. You know it's got 'Mary' carved on the butt. She's the sweetest little rifle on the front—I've kept her in good shape."

Then Jim went down the trench. Staring into the darkness, I thought of him in his most typical position, lying on his belly behind a leaping machine gun, joy in his face, his preoccupations so great that his hands seemed to melt into the grips.

They got Jim early the next afternoon. He was lying ahead of me, always crawling a little forward, always keeping a watchful eye on his section. The machine gun at our left jammed; Jim, who understood guns better than anyone else in the battalion, started worming toward it through the stubble. As he crossed a little rise of ground, something spoke from the fascist trenches and machine gun bullets cut the ground around him. Jim shuddered as though he were cold, tried to rise, then dropped and lay still.

A First Aid man sprinted out, grabbed him and hauled him back. Bullets searched the stubble as we examined the wound. Blood seeped out through the little black smudge between the ribs. "Wind coming through," muttered the First Aid man. "He's done for."

Jim was not quite conscious for several minutes. At first he just asked for water; then he cried in a voice like a girl's that the planes were coming, and his whole body shook. His eyes opened and he looked the First Aid man in the face. His voice was weak and calm. "Am I leaving?" he asked, and the First Aid man answered, "Guess you are, kid."

"Hell," said Jim "Well . . . somehow there isn't much to say. Tell Mary I love her . . ." pause of half a minute . . . "You boys run the fascists out of here" . . . a longer pause . . . "Help me with my fist, kid." I saw what he was trying to do, and I placed his clenched fist to his forehead in the People's Front salute. His voice was tired. "*Salud*, comrades" and he lay back with closed eyes, waiting.

We had a little rest two days later. We moved away then from the field where Jim lay. Perhaps, I thought, he has been buried by now; if not, it's not Jim anymore, just a bundle of rags, among dozens of bundles of rags. It was the life in him which made him Jim, different from all the others, and that life was gone now.

I started to write to Mary. Date. Spain. "Dear Mary" . . . No, "Dear Comrade" was better. I mused for several minutes, than realized I must be half asleep. "Dear Comrade Mary" would do.

And now what? All sorts of ideas ran through my mind, how I could break the news gently, with what touching phrases I could assuage her grief. But everything seemed badly formed and clumsy.

I crammed the paper in my pocket and lay down on the ground. I couldn't write it when I was half asleep like this. Maybe, I could wake up before it got too dark to write. I felt dull and heavy. My eyes closed and great waves of slumber swirled over me. I hugged closer to my side the rifle Jim had named Mary, and then fell asleep.

LOVE AND REVOLUTIONARY GREETINGS

A Mother in Spain

The Lincoln Battalion was luxuriating in relief. We needed rest. We'd been a long time on the line in Jarama.

Months stretch out on the front. When I first climbed the bitter Jarama hills the rainy season was still on. A grey haze of rain and mist hid those first terrible days, shrouding the bayonet charges and the beating machine guns and the surging tanks. Well, the fascists had been stopped. Picked German and Italian shock troops had been thrown back by a third their number. We had dug trenches; while we held the trenches, the Madrid-Valencia highway was safe. Glorious Madrid, the Spaniards call her. Impregnable Madrid! And we were guarding her lifeline.

We guarded that line a good while. The haze of rain went away and a haze of heat took its place. Spring threw a crimson Spanish shawl of poppies over the grey rocks. Slowly the crimson became rusty and the shawl tattered. But now we had relief, far from the hissing of bullets and the crash of guns. We looked at the green fields, drank *vino*, tried to talk Spanish with the girls—and rested.

We were quartered in a tiny town by a white stream where the girls washed clothes. The hills on each side rolled green almost as far as one could see, then merged into barren mountains. Tiny white plaster huts, shaped like an architect's design for a beehive were scattered through the ravines. Three kilometers down the valley lay another town a trifle larger than ours.

"They're having a dance down at the next town," Paul told me.

I closed my book and looked up. "When?"

"Tonight. A bunch of the Cuban boys are going, and I'm going with them. Want to come?"

The road was beautiful in the sunset. This was harvest season. Boys, old men, girls and women, with here and there a middle-aged farmer, were still cutting the grain. With all the young men at the front and a heavy crop this year, it was a big job: the whole family worked from sunrise to sunset. It was a patriotic act to work hard in the fields for the Government had proclaimed that not an acre must be left uncut. "A hoe is as valuable as a rifle, a plow as a machine gun," say the posters scattered through the villages of loyal Spain. Many soldiers help the farmers harvest the grain during their periods of leave.

We saluted the workers in the fields, and they answered with the clenched fist or raised sickle. Everybody salutes in Spain. We saluted the old women driving two-wheeled carts, pulled by tiny donkeys, ragged at the edges like poorly stuffed mohair chairs. We saluted with appropriate remarks and compliments the long line of pretty girls from the village, who, arm in arm, strolled along the middle of the road and made the donkey carts get out of the way.

The dance was in full swing when we got there. The music was provided by a tuneless barrel organ, which was hammering out popular songs. It was the People's House headquarters of the General Workers' Union and recreation center for the whole town.

Our eight Cubans swung into action immediately. There were plenty of girls dancing together, for the boys of the village were scattered in battalions on every front in Spain. This was a good working class village, an old man told us proudly; every healthy man who could be spared had volunteered. A few of them were home on leave. We saw them dancing—happy, strong young men, made much of by the girls.

Johnny, a corporal in the Cuban section, began a flirtation with a pretty girl in red: Manuel, the orator and spokesman of the group gathered a number of older men around him and explained why we of the International Brigade had come to Spain. The audience listened approvingly, now and then asking questions. The rest of the Cuban boys flitted from flower to flower, dancing to the crazy tunes with first one girl and then another. Paul and I couldn't dance, Spanish method, so we stood by and enjoyed the color, the din and the furious turmoil of it all.

The dance kept on for a couple of hours. Then groups began sifting away. There was wheat to cut in the morning.

Manuel, excited, rounded us up. We saw Johnny demur— evidently he preferred to stay with the girl with the red dress as long as possible—but Manual whispered something in his ear and he left her with ceremony and joined us.

"Tortillas!" explained Manuel. "I have found out where some of the best tortillas are made." We trooped after him.

The house had two burlap sacks over the door as curtains. Embroidered on them was a large red star and some rabbits marching up and down. The stairs were dark; but when we reached the kitchen-dining room at the top, there was a blaze of warmth. Over the fire, pumping the old hand-bellows stooped a woman who looked anywhere from eighty up. Her face was wrinkled like a dry prune and her eyes always seemed tearful. At the table stood an old man, much more hearty than the woman, but still shaky on his legs, peeling potatoes.

Manuel presented the situation briefly. Here were gallant comrades, who had volunteered to fight for Spain against Hitler and Mussolini. They had spent months on the front without tasting a tortilla. Now we had heard that her tortillas were the best in miles, and we would like to purchase tortillas for all present.

The situation about eggs was discussed. At first the old woman was afraid there were not enough eggs; then she decided there might be if she used potatoes in the tortillas. Finally she went to look, and in a little while mysterious preparations had begun to sizzle in the long-handled frying pan.

Meantime we sat around on toppling chairs while the old man brought us anise and *vino* with two glasses, one for each, which we kept constantly passing. All except Francisco. He was a big man, a good soldier; it seemed a little incongruous to see him sitting here intently peeling potatoes and onions.

Johnny, a little heated with the anise was telling the story of how a man he knew in New York got hurt. "I said to him," explained Johnny, "you called me all kinds of bad names" (he gave a list) "and I take it. But now when you call me a son-of-a-bitch that insults my mother. I love my mother, and any son-of-a-bitch goddamn son-of-a-bitch that calls me a son-of-a-bitch is going to get it hard."

Then Manuel came over to us very gravely. "Boys, you know what they tell me? They tell me that this woman here, she only had two sons, and she loses them both for the Spanish Republic. The one is killed at our front, Jarama: the other at Madrid. I think we should get up in a solemn tribute to the two sons of this mother."

We stood with bowed heads for a minute or two, the old woman standing before us crying without a sound. She looked utterly frail, yet I thought then there was something about her quite unbeaten. Then Manuel said with his sweep of the hands: "Comrades, I have something to propose. This old woman, she had lost her sons for freedom. I think we should make her the mother of the Cuban Section of the Lincoln Brigade."

One by one we went forward to kiss her. She was not crying now, but hugged each of us passionately, kissing us three or four times. Then, tears flowing again, she went back to her tortillas.

They were a long time coming, but when they came they were wonderful. One onion and one potato tortilla apiece, and either showed us what food could taste like. The old man sat at the table with us and told us how he was the first Republican in the district, and what trouble the King and Church gave him in those days.

"Well," proposed Paul finally, after the last of the tortillas had been consumed and the last of the *vino* drunk, "well, shall we go?"

"Let us go," said Manuel, "but first we pay our mama and kiss her goodbye."

"No pay!" insisted the old man; but Johnny shoved three ten-peseta bills in his pocket. The old fellow fumbled with them; dropped them; then picked them up, trembling with gratitude.

The old woman did not cry when we kissed her. But when Manuel came back to kiss her again, enfolding her in his arms in an extravagant gesture, she looked up.

"Alfonso and Juan, they wanted to chase the fascists out," she said. "But they are both dead. Will you chase the fascists?"

We swore we would.

Well, Manuel is dead now; Johnny was shot in the arm but it healed quickly and now he is corporal in Manuel's place. Paul is at a hospital some place with a bad one in the body; here I am in hospital, too.

Out in the field some place is the Cuban Section of the Lincoln Battalion. They run a few steps forward drop and fire. They are keeping faith with their mother.[1]

1. Private collection.

11

April–July 1937

More Letters Home

D EAR CLARA,
　　　T. S. Eliot remarks that "April is the cruelest month" etc.
I haven't anything against the month but the weather which ac-
companies it is variable. I found a fish in my pocket this morning;
this afternoon I'm going to put him on a hot rock to fry, and what
I don't eat now I'll set out to freeze tonight.

Despite the weather we've been having a swell time. April 14
is Republic Day, I think, and celebrations are being held from the
front lines to the mountain villages. I ought to have a good time. I
pal around with the craziest bunch of guys this patient nation has
ever endured. When they were up at the front they used to go over
on grenade parties and bring back machine guns; and when they
brought back one which wouldn't work they wanted to return it
that night. Now they've been recuperating from wounds and ter-
rorizing the barbers but the populace is indulgent towards them.
The workers look at the International Brigade with a kindly eye
and treat the boys to *vino tinto* and my, my, it is lousy stuff to get
drunk on.

Don't worry too much about Mrs. Simpson's divorce; I have
consulted His Majesty's Ambassador and every effort is being
made to change the date.

Are you keeping up with your reading? I'm not, but I should be.

R. P.

Dear Mother,

Got your first letter yesterday and it made me feel very good. Not that there was a vast amount of news but it was swell to hear that everyone is okay except Billy who's getting a little lame. Tell him to quit chasing cats in his next incarnation.

I think from now on I'll be getting letters regularly, which will be very nice. I enjoy the dual role of a roamer who ignores his family responsibilities and a family man who sits still half an hour every evening and thinks of home. However, to carry out this last I need letters to prove to me that there is such a place as home.

Kidding aside, it really is very nice to get news from you. Send me a good bit of news about what's happening politically, especially locally: Ohio, C.I.O. and Workers' Alliance's strike news. Don't bother writing any news on the Spanish situation. If you want to send me anything send clippings.

I've been collecting a book of revolutionary songs from every place. I now have Irish, Spanish, Yankee, French and a few extra languages which I do not understand. I'm handicapped by lack of languages, singing ability and knowledge of how to write notes, so I don't expect it to be anything remarkable when I'm done, but still it's lots of fun. I have a theory that songs have never been really utilized except by the Wobblies in America. Here they sing all the time.

I'm sending a letter for Max in this package. The air raid I talk about was when I was on the way to where I am now. I'm so far from the front now that I haven't seen a plane in quite a while.

Love,
R. P.
Spain

Dear Max,

I apologize for not writing sooner and oftener. There has been a good deal to report but seldom the time and sometimes not even the tools to report it with. I was rather incorrect in my last letter when I stated that I was in a factory. In consulting my notes, I find I've been on the front since the middle of February. We had some extremely hot fighting at that time, and lost quite a few good Comrades. I want to mention especially an S.P. member, Paul Niepold of Brookwood Labor College. He went out from the trench to get in a wounded Comrade and they plugged him in the chest. Any of the boys who knew him will agree that he was one of the best comrades on the front.

But now things have gotten very quiet on this front. All we hear is an occasional explosive bullet smashing itself on the sandbags. They're ugly things—leave a little hole where they go in and a big jagged hole where they leave. We haven't lost a man for weeks. We can afford to wait a little while because by all indications the fascists are getting weaker, and I can see that we are getting stronger myself. Still this machine-gun business is getting tiresome and I'll be glad when we've cleaned the bastards out and can go home. There's lots of work to be done in America.

It is rather difficult for me to appraise the political situation. From the military standpoint I think, from what I can see with my own eyes, that the fascists are smashed and will soon be on the run, though it may take a good bit more blood to mop them up. From the political standpoint, however, our only direct contact is with our Spanish comrades in the trenches; and even this is fragmentary, because we don't know Spanish well.

I should make another qualification as well; that in this fighting I have frequently come into contact with other working-class parties. For this discussion I'll refer specifically to the Communist Party. I have been strongly impressed first, by the behavior of many of the Communist comrades, their absolute self sacrifice and revolutionary courage; and more important, the smooth working organization which they put to work on any subject which they are convinced is vital to the workers' cause. In this respect the Socialist Party has still lessons to learn from the C.P. I have become the strongest possible partisan of a United Front with the S.P.A. on every possible issue—not such a United Front as would sacrifice our principals or subordinate our theoretical differences (the genuine United Front would not tend to do that) but an escape from the unfortunate purist attitude which some locals of our Party hold. If the Communists and Socialists can unite on the issue of going over the top together in the face of machine gun fire—if Paul Niepold could get killed helping a wounded Communist, and another Communist could risk his life to bring in both the wounded and the dead man—then I can see no difficulty in both parties participating, and *participating actively*, in the North American Committee at home.

I suppose that my opinion on the Catalonian revolt should be considered in the light of this qualification.

Our first feeling (this includes myself) in reading of the fighting in Barcelona was of acute discomfort. Here we were hundreds of miles in Spain fighting a vicious enemy which would have taken the first sign of dissension as a signal to attack. We knew we could handle the bastards and drive them back as long as we got bullets, food and men on the line—but wouldn't the inevitable result of large-scale fighting in the rear the cutting off of supplies. Our army contained men of every tendency—did these revolutionists want us in the front to rage against each other? Moreover, events had shown that there was a tendency for the POUM to accept members without investigation, which certainly gave members of Franco's Fifth Column an excellent chance. I personally was convinced that even if the POUM rebellion were to succeed the revolutionary aims of it would be sabotaged by the hidden fascists within it.

Hence the feeling of every man on the line, when the news came that the revolt had been suppressed, was one of extreme relief. I had the opinion that the severe suppression of the POUM which followed was not only justified but well overdue. This is not to say that I, as a revolutionary Socialist would not prefer to serve under a revolutionary government, though my confidence in the POUM is not such that I would want that body to control it. But what about my Catholic comrade in the Basque region, who wants only regional autonomy? What about my anarchist comrade on the right, whose life has been devoted to fighting against government and who presumably would not welcome the vast governmental powers of a dictatorship of the proletariat? What about the great masses in the Socialist and Communist Parties, who want a revolutionary government but are against fighting for one at the present time. These soldiers, workers and peasants cannot be controlled by any *coup d'etat;* they must be convinced, and I feel that this convincing can take effect in action only after the war is over and then quite probably through peaceful means.

Thus I do not feel that the S.P.U.S.A. was correct in condemning Largo Cabellero's government for suppressing the Trotskyites. I would in fact have preferred it had the situation been favorable to suppressing them more completely so that this revolt could have been avoided. In the light of what I have seen in Spain I consider their slogan—that we may win the war yet lose the revolution—to be fundamentally incorrect. A great number of the large capitalists aided Franco, so that many factories are now in the hands of the workers. The land seems to be chiefly owned by the peasants, making the strongest possible bulwark against Franco. To push collectivized agriculture at this time would be Utopian. I didn't recall Lenin having advanced collectivized agriculture during the civil war.

One other point in which the Trotskyites were mistaken when I left, and may still be mistaken—the amount of aid given by Soviet Russia to the Spanish Republic.

Personally I have been somewhat disappointed by the news admittedly scant of the Socialist Party in the U.S.A. I hope strongly that the Party is built up in organizational strength, and that it starts working in closer collaboration with other working-class groups. I see no reason why our Trotskyite comrades should not remain in the Party, but I think we must insist that they respect Party discipline and adhere to the Party line. I want to make it clear that I am not one of those who pronounce Trotskyite with a hiss. I consider the Trotskyites as my comrades, but so do I consider as comrades fighting trade unionists, militant pacifists, and others whose line I do not agree with. The Trotskyite line, as I saw it in action in Spain, is extremely bad. I would consider it a great favor if you would pass this on to the Party members and Yipsels, so that the majority of them got a chance to see it. I realize that you may not share many of the conclusions I put forward in the political section, but here it is a case of an absent Yipsel who is extremely anxious to have his voice heard, and I guess the job falls on you. If you get a chance, read it at a meeting. I'd like to hear some of the comments if you could write them to me.

If not, try to write anyway. I want to hear from the old gang, and you especially.

Fraternally yours,
Sam

Dear Clara,

Kid, I've been having a swell time lately. That's due chiefly to having gotten two letters, one from Mother and one from you, on the same day. I was away at school at the time, learning something technical and I guess they must have chased me all over Spain before they found me. They were given that afternoon to one of the kids, and that night after I was in bed he remembered that he had a letter, and gave me Mother's. (He remembered yours next day.) All the lights were out in the joint, so I went groping around the town for an hour and finally found a lighted candle.

I'm answering your letter this late because I already wrote one and lost it, and then they sent me back from school to the place I work, and then I decided to write out a few of those songs and send them along. Which I did. They tell me that I.R.A song is being sung a good bit by the boys on the front just now. They put special emphasis on the business about Mary kind and pure, because the front tends to make people sentimental. It is astonishing the number of marriages which have been concluded by mail from this country, though they were generally previously consummated, I guess.

I have given up hope of ever getting out of this joint and getting a crack at the front. I don't think the Spanish government trains men and then withdraws them. I suppose I'm doing valuable work, but it's slightly disgusting.

Somehow I can't muster much disappointment about absence making your heart grow fonder. In fact, if you have a gross or so of snapshots of yourself, it would be nice if you could export one to Spain. I feel sure that I'll find a market for it among the local populace or if worse comes to the worst I'll take it off your hands myself. At home I always considered this business of photographs as strictly the bunk. I still do but most of the boys have photos of a sweetheart or wife, sometimes five or six of them; and the Levingers were always conventional. What I mean is, don't bother having one taken, but if you can spare one I'd like it.

Yesterday was my birthday. I am now twenty years old, and have a mustache, which is bushy at one end. I think I'm doing fairly well. I also read a stray copy of T. S. Eliot's poems. He is not a Marxist.

This is practically all the International News which we furnish with our regular service. Our supplemental service consists of simple rumors, official rumors and rumors with gold stripes and walking canes. Write me again, and I'll send you a few of them.

How are the vegetables in the back garden doing? Have the beans I planted come up yet?

Love to Mother, Father, Aunt Eva and the rest. Joseph, too.

Joy to the world,
Sam

Dear Father,

Everything's going fine, splendid and wonderful. I'm on the trail of my typewriter and have hopes of getting it back by the end of the war. I learned two new songs and forgot three old ones which puts me one ahead of the game. The weather is bloody lovely, pretty hot with occasional dust clouds. All the bushes are getting covered with yellow flowers, although the thorns are still present if you brush against them. We can see some big snowy mountains a long ways off when the weather is clear. Moreover from all the news we hear we seem to be winning the war pretty much all around, although I don't know what Mussolini would say to that. There is a rumor that after his defeat in Guadalajara he sent a protest to the League of Nations claiming that Italian citizens were being molested on Spanish soil.

The paper of the International Brigade, *Voice of the Fighter* says that Mussolini was indignant when he was told that Guadalajara proved that Italians were poor soldiers. "Why, they're the best soldiers in Spain! Look at the Garibaldi Battalion!" (Mussolini always uses exclamation points.)

Our letters seem to be getting back and forth pretty quickly. In fact, the round trip takes only a month which certainly isn't long.

I haven't met the boys from Columbus yet. If I know any of them have Clara write me the first name and initials. Although from the news SB of the Socialist Party, U.S.A., thought not much can be done to Americans in Spain. Except refuse them protection. Personally I'm going to see the American consul and demand a battleship to protect me.

Write or cable when one of Mother's chickens lays an egg. Also try to put off fixing the garage roof till I can be home to do it right.

Love,
R. P.

Levinger family passport, 1931

Sam in front of map of Spain, 1937

Sam with his machine gun company, Spain 1937

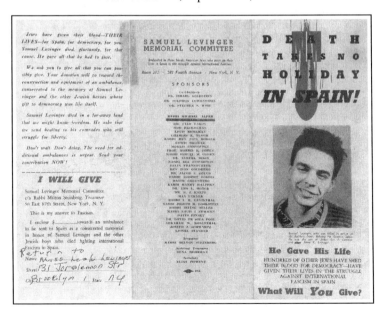

Death certificate, September 6, 1937

Samuel Levinger Memorial Committee flyer

Belchite 2010

Church in Belchite

Belchite, December 2010

12

American Medical Bureau in Spain

D R. EDWARD Barsky, the chief of the American Medical Bureau in Spain, left a lucrative surgical practice in New York City to head up the team of doctors and nurses who volunteered for Spain. Here he describes conditions in a mobile field hospital set up in winter to treat the wounded at the Battle of Jarama. Conditions in other field hospitals on other fronts were as bad. Or worse.

DR. EDWARD BARSKY

In front of the hospital were our new ambulances loaded with wounded soldiers. (A thing long expected, planned for; now it was almost a shocking surprise). The faces of the soldiers were gray; their torn clothes the color of earth. The wounds were of types we had never seen before: ghastly ones of the skull, the abdomen, the extremities, parts of legs and arms blown off—skull fractures—a limb all out of shape with a broken shaft of bone sticking out of a red gash.

Mostly they were young, yet some were really old; Americans, French, Germans and Spaniards, groaning, (*Ay-a, mi madre!*) or just lying there quietly biting their lips, with pale faces and anxious eyes that followed every movement of doctor or nurse.

Ambulance after ambulance came in. The entire town came out and gathered around, getting the first real impact of the war. For this was a forgotten town, near enough to the front lines to be shaken by their thunder, yet hidden from the highways; it had heard war but never seen it. We had been like that, too!

Having crowds was bad. It interfered with the work of getting patients out of the ambulances. If an enemy plane should pass over, the pilot's attention would be attracted by the crowd and there would be bombing. A few words to the *Alcalde* (Mayor) and then the town crier went through the little cobbled streets warning the people to stay home and we had no more trouble.

Soon every bed in our hospital was taken; extra mattresses donated by the townspeople were thrown in the halls and these also were filled. Other patients were accommodated on stretchers. The floor space was solid with them; we even put up benches. There was barely enough room to move around. Where was the gleaming emptiness now?

Cold. Bitter, damp cold that froze our blood. What of the wounded?

In the icy triage or admitting room the wounded were quickly sorted. Many were in shock, some because of their severe wounds and some from exposure. These were treated with warm fluids. Then we invented something: we put a cold patient on a stretcher, covered him with blankets, which hung to the ground, underneath we put a primus stove and cooked him gently.

The operating staff went into action immediately. The operating room seemed colder than any other spot. The tiny trickle of precious water which came from our water jars was only a long icicle and it required a great deal of determination to scrub conscientiously. The sterile gown was wet, the powder inside the rubber gloves was slimy. Each instrument made the hand ache as in handling ice.

We started a stretch of work which lasted for forty hours.[1]

1. Barsky and Waugh, "The Surgeon Goes to War," 4–5.

13

August 1937

Tell Them I'm Lonely

SAM

MADRID, AUGUST 1, 1937

We have been having more fun than a picnic lately, with machine-guns playing *no pasarán*, and bombing planes five times a day instead of meals. It all ended up with me in a nice comfortable hospital. I don't say a safe hospital, because Nazi bombs have an unhappy ability to drop right through the hospital skylight, while the plane is searching for some military objective ten miles away. The Madrid papers show a fascist pilot pointing to the cross on top of the hospital and remarking, "There's the objective". The cartoon isn't so far wrong either.

If there is any point that should be brought out, it is that we're not fighting Spanish patriots intent on rejuvenating Spain, nor are we fighting priests and nuns. I know lots of Spaniards intent on rejuvenating Spain, but they're all in the People's Army. As for the priest, a good friend of mine was among that group. He was in the Spanish section of our battalion, a corporal; and he did well until an explosive bullet tore his arm off. Now he's doing work in the rear. An excellent comrade.

We're fighting against Italians, Germans and Moors, and they're damn good fighters on the average, too. With the exception of the Moors, who enjoy a close-quartered scrap, they won't stand up to close fighting with grenades and bayonets; but the pity of it is, they have so many machine guns that it is often hard to come near them. The Lincoln Battalion found out that on several occasions in Jarama.

Since our showing in this Sierra campaign the Lincoln Battalion is considered as crack shock troops. They rush us to the position, show us the enemy, and let us draw our own conclusions. Fighting is the most tiring business I know, and in my opinion the battalion has performed feats of endurance to rank with the ten thousand Greeks of what's-his-name.

The point however, is that this has lost all semblance of a civil war and has become a straight Italo-German invasion. From the progressive's point of view it is something which must be resisted to the end, because it is an invasion of People's Spain, a Spain where the workers have most of the say. And from a Socialist's point of view Spain is worthy of every sacrifice, for here is a people who are being attacked by international Fascism largely because they have attempted to move forward toward economic change.

I wish I could express in words what I feel about this people. It is a gallant, charming people, making the greatest individual sacrifices in order that the nation may continue free. It's not an easy thing to smash a people like this with artillery and bombers. The *fascistas* are trying it, and they're getting plenty of support from the "democratic" governments, but I'd bet my rifle and cartridge belt they don't succeed.

We need help, though, and plenty of it. We need it in the form of material contributions, sympathy and international organization. The fascists are getting away with a lot because our side of the case isn't really understood in places like Liverpool, England and Columbus, Ohio. We'll let the English take care of Liverpool, but you folks see what you can do about Columbus. Clara Distel is the head of the committee in Columbus; anyway you can cooperate with her, and with the North American Committee to Aid Spanish Democracy, without of course putting yourself on the spot; it would pay big dividends. We're going to win here all right, but international aid can save many lives by shortening the war, and that includes women and children getting buried in houses by bombs.

And I'd very much like you to write, telling me your impressions of what's happening in the States—here we get chiefly the triumphant blasts of *The Daily Worker*. I'd like to get some other slant, too. In fact, get lots of people to write to me. My address is Samuel Levinger, Rm. 17.1, Soccoro Rojo International, Albecete, Spain. Tell them I'm lonely.

> Fraternally yours,
> Samuel Levinger

SAM

I wrote this poem in the hospital after I was wounded at the Battle of Brunete.

The War is Long

Comrades, the battle is bloody, the war is long:
Across grey hills ahead hear the shout of the guns;
Above us sweep white planes pregnant with pain:
See the tanks sullen and savage, hating flesh:
And listen—the rifles are pointing men out for oblivion:

The winging machine guns are beating the drums of death.
Comrades, the battle is bloody, the war is long:
There lies a comrade, head swathed in blood and bandages:
There stands a broken comrade with white face twitching;
There lie our dead, waiting for a little sand.
And we are tired with war and sick with danger.
Dreaming of girls waiting a long ways off:

And there is blood on our hands we cannot wash clean.
Blood on our souls which will not wash off for a long time.
Comrades, the battle is bloody, the war is long:

Still let us climb the grey hill and charge the guns.
Pressing with lean bayonets toward the slopes beyond.
Soon those who are still living will see green grass.
A free bright country shining with a star:
And those who charged the guns will be remembered:
And from red blood white pinnacles shall tower.

SAM

Dear Comrade Distel,

Nothing much doing now. I've been in a hospital in Madrid for a couple of weeks. There's nothing the matter with me, but I guess some doctor thinks there must be, and a vacation is always welcome to a person of my temperament.

I think we should soon see a big push which will clear the center section. In the Sierra campaign we proved ourselves to have far more manpower than the fascists, and generally speaking of better quality; but they still have more artillery than we do, and more planes, though ours are far superior.

I suppose Dayton will soon be experiencing what a union is like. We many see very rapid growth soon both there and in Columbus. I wish I was there to see it, but this is also interesting.

If you get time drop me a note in one of Clara's letters. Tell me the details of the steel strike outcome—here we're not sure yet whether it won or lost. And have you any news of Ohio Worker's Alliance? If you run across Marty, or Louis Moon I'd like them to write me too.

My address is Samuel Levinger, Rm 17.1, Socorro Rojo, Albacete, Spain.

Fraternally yours,
Samuel Levinger

Dear Clara,

Not much to say except that I love you and have been behaving myself. Sending a couple of cigarette holders, one for you and one for Mother, guaranteed to break you of the cigarette habit in short order. Will write as soon as possible.

Love,
Samuel

SAM

It was all very pleasant in the hospital being kept nice and clean, getting almost enough to eat, nothing to do but write letters and work on a journal I had written months before that I thought could be sold to *The Citizen*. I wrote our family doctor and left the letter lying open so my nurse would read the opening paragraph: "The hospitals in Spain are understaffed, but everybody rushes around so fast that this deficiency is partly made up. Do the doctors frown on nurses kissing all the patients in America? Here they don't." I wrote and told Clara that I had just finished rereading *Vanity Fair* and I think that she has more loyalty than Becky Sharpe, more brains than Amelia. But I didn't mention to anyone that since I'd been wounded twice, a slight wound in the hand in the early days at Jarama, now this serious concussion, I'd been ordered home.

"You can do more back there," Hans Amalie, my commander, insisted. "You know it's the rule—two wounds and back you go! You can talk and write. You can tell people back in America what they don't know—get us money for smokes and comforts for the boys. Get those fellows in Washington to lift the Embargo. You've got to go back."

"Sure," I agreed with him. "I've got to go back."

As soon as I was able to walk I deserted from the hospital. A few days later I scribbled this note home:

Dear Mother,

I'm now with the battalion after a trip which puts that of What-you-may-call-'em and his ten thousand Greeks in the shade. For four days I only ate bread and fruit. Grapes (blue and green), figs (blue, red and yellow), peaches, apples etc. Then a Spanish battalion took me in and showered me with kindness and mutton chops. They claimed that the Internationals were deserving of all credit because we had left home to fight Fascism instead of waiting till it got around to us. I rode on a train for a while with a bunch of POUM boys, swell kids, who fed me with red peppers. They explained their position, which did not sound much better in Spanish than in English. They were conscripted from Catalonia, going to the front after a pretty good period of training.

The battalion is doing fine here, although it's pretty warm. It feels fine to be eating the battalion food again, and also to have some practice in English, a language I thought I'd forgotten.

In a place where I was just staying I got hold of *The Frogs* by Aristophanes, one of those little blue books like you had at home; wouldn't it be funny if it was one of the books you wrote you were going to send to Spain for the Lincolns? I'm going to read it after I have a swim in the creek. Don't worry if I don't get a chance to write again for a few days—there's nothing much happening here, anyway.[1]

SAM

I do not fear that blankness that men call death,
Nor say set prayers to baffle a vague-guessed doom,
Nor gaze with sick despair at the enveloping
Black bowels of the tomb.

My life is joyous with purple verse and clouds,
Ships I have sailed on, beer that I have spilled;
Forward lies struggle and hope, a world to destroy,
A new world to build.

And when my eyes begin to flutter and close
I shall be sad; but why should my courage shake?
If there is darkness beyond, why then, I will sleep,
If light, I shall wake.[2]

1. E. Levinger, *Death in the Mountains*, 172.
2. Private collection.

14

August 24–September 7, 1937

Battle of Belchite

S TEVE NELSON was at Belchite when Sam was there. In *The Volunteers* he describes the battle.

STEVE NELSON

Napoleon tired to capture Belchite once, and he had failed. Several Loyalist commanders tried and were stopped by a powerfully built defense system prepared by Nazi engineers, with traditional German thoroughness. They advanced a little, advanced and died, and advanced again; they broke through many defenses, but still more defenses remained. The city held stubbornly. The city was strong.

Belchite could not be captured, but Belchite had to be captured, for several reasons. Barcelona believed it had already fallen; to tell Barcelona otherwise now would have a very bad effect on Barcelona morale; and Barcelona was the industrial center of Spain. Production of guns, trucks, munitions, shoes, and clothes for the army fluctuated as Barcelona morale fluctuated. This, on the political side.

Military considerations were certainly no less pressing. The bulk of the attacking force had driven deep into fascist territory. Belchite was behind them, a powerful threat so long as it remained in fascist hands. On the positive side, Belchite lay on a road leading straight to Saragossa. Capture of the city would open a new route for attack.

To Charlie the Sniper, Ruby Ryant, all the Joes and Bills and Eds and Dicks lying in a shallow trench under the walls of Belchite, these matters were by no means clear. They did know that any man who raised up six inches off the ground was going to get a fascist bullet through him. They knew the trench was straight instead of zigzag, so the snipers in the houses at the left were able to enfilade it. They knew the sun was hot, even so early in the morning. It looked like a long, unhappy day ahead, lying there glued to the ground, not daring to move a muscle.

They had moved up at night, in to the trench, which was not a prepared trench, but a shallow ditch running out at an angle from the edge of town. The night before, the houses overlooking the ditch had been empty, but in the darkness, the fascists had come back, and set up machine guns, and posted snipers in windows overlooking the ditch . . .

I was on duty. I listened, made notes, and went out to the anti-tank battery.

The little guns were sleek and beautiful. You aimed them like a rifle, and the velocity of their shell was so great that the shell traveled upwards of two miles in a straight line, without drop . . .

"They are the finest weapons used on either side in Spain, these anti-tank guns were made in the Soviet Union," the commander of the battery, an Englishman named Slate, boasted. "Put a few shells into the windows of the houses on the left down there, will you?" I asked him. I made a sketch, indicating which houses and which windows.

The battery commander said, "Sure." He saw me staring at the gun. "Want to try it once?"

I looked through a ground-glass screen, like the finder on a camera, marked with cross hairs. I turned a crank, and the screen moved. The houses were suddenly very close. The cross hairs bore on a window. Inside the room, I could see someone moving, and the sleek barrel of a machine gun.

The gun said, 'Wham!' the window was filled with flame and white smoke, and then the explosion was heard.

On the ground under the muzzles, wet canvas was stretched, so the blast from the muzzles wouldn't kick up a whirlwind of dust for observers to spot. The same technique, I remembered, Charlie the Sniper had used.

I went back to headquarters. Behind me, the guns kept talking, methodically clearing the row of houses of machine-gun nests.

Bob was yelling into the phone. "You've got to!" Bob was bellowing. "I say you've got to, you hear?"

He slammed the earpiece back onto the hook, and glared at me. "Hicks says he can't go forward. Steve, one of us two has got to go up there and do something." I looked at Bob, his right arm still in a sling from the wounds he got at Jarama and I said, "I'll go."

The battalion post was a hastily improvised dugout in a dry wash. Hicks' temper was fully as bad as Bob's. "What the hell is the matter with you guys?' he shouted at me. 'What do you think we are? Go forward—how can we go forward? The town's bristling with machine guns, thick as hair on dog's back, and you want to send infantry against them! You want to slaughter the whole damn battalion? Where's the artillery?"

"I wouldn't know," I said. "But I do know the guys can't stay where they are. The anti-tanks can't stay around all day shooting snipers out of windows for us. They'll be back pretty soon, and—"

"I don't know what you expect us to do. It's murder, sending the boys up against machine guns, I'd like to know who the hell cooked up this bloody mess, the whole thing's a botch, one mistake after another—"

He was a brave man, and honest, and kindly, and he hated the thought of the men of his command getting killed in a helpless, hopeless attack against protected machine guns. He knew the battalion could not go forward. He was thinking about what could and could not be done.

But beyond the question of what can be done is always the question of what must be done. The boys must not stay in that trench, to be picked off like ducks in a pond. Ground already gained must be held, and even if that were not true, a retirement over bare ground would cost more lives than an attack. No safety lay in retreat.

Therefore the battalion must go forward.[1]

ELMA

Years ago I'd taught Sam not to believe everything he read. This was proven true again, even about something as concrete as death. Because there are several accounts of Sam's death. But even eyewitness reports can be wrong:

Robert Rosenstone in *Crusade of the Left* describes Sam's death: "Close to the cathedral on all sides now, the Americans, supported by a Spanish battalion, tried to rush across the open plaza toward the building, but they were driven back by withering enemy fire. They regrouped in nearby buildings and then tried a second assault that also failed. These were costly maneuvers and

---

1. Nelson, *The Volunteers*, 181–84.

among the men who fell dead in them were Henry Eaton and Samuel Levinger . . .".[2]

Peter Carroll described the battle: "The six-day siege also claimed Henry Eaton, who thought it ironic that the fascists always seemed to make their last stand inside churches, and Samuel Levinger, son of a rabbi and a student leader from Ohio State University, who had a premonition that he 'would not come out . . . alive.'"[3]

Cecil Eby in *Between the Bullet and the Lie*: "Very quickly they learned that Belchite would not be a scrimmage like Quinto. Houses tightly ringed the town with the compactness of solid wall, and each window harbored a sniper. Within minutes a harrowing fire beat down upon them and stopped their advance. One of the first Americans killed was Sam Levinger, YIPSEL poet from Ohio."[4]

In mid-September, a couple of weeks after the battle was over Robert Hale Merriman, the chief of staff of the Abraham Lincoln Brigade, and his wife, Marion, visited Belchite. Marion Merriman described what they saw in her book *American Commander in Spain*.

> As Bob explained the battle to me, walking through the town's ruins, the shadows lengthened across the empty fields nearby. Here one of our best machine-gunners fell, beside that wall Burt was killed, there was Dany's grave, here Sidney fell, a sniper's bullet between his eyes, there Steve Nelson was wounded. Our losses were actually very low, but they included some of the best and most loved of our men.
>
> As we passed a little factory huge sewer rats scurried into a drain beside the road. They were as large as cats. Even though it was two weeks later, the smell of burned

2. Rosenstone, *Crusade of the Left*, 208.

3. Carroll, *The Odyssey of the Abraham Lincoln Brigade*, 157.

4. Eby, *Between the Bullet and the Lie*, 160.

flesh still hung faint and nauseating in the cool dusk. Their forces far outnumbered ours, but the fascists had not even attempted to dispose of their dead. They had left hundreds of decaying corpses stacked in various buildings . . .

As we passed through the debris-filled streets, the air of desolation and death deepened. Homeless cats scuttled about, hungry, and dogs howled and fought bitterly down the blackness of narrow streets. The full moon was bright by the time we reached the cathedral at the center. Across its worn stone steps limply lay a purple and white Falangist banner. Further down was a priest's cassock, perhaps shed in flight.

Only the square admitted enough light for Bob and me to read the fascist posters still stuck to broken walls, posters depicting the horrors of Marxism rather than the horrors of the war that a small group of fascists had started. I noticed there were posted rules for the modesty of young women, rules requiring long skirts and long sleeves, saying sin is a woman's because she tempts man. There were no posters promising a government for all the people.[5]

5. Merriman and Lerude, *American Commander in Spain*, 169.

15

September 1937

Field Hospital, La Puebla de Hijar

B UT, IN fact, Sam did not die on the battlefield at Belchite. He had been critically wounded and was taken by ambulance to the field hospital at La Puebla de Hijar.

CECIL EBY

At La Puebla de Hijar the medical staff had to convert a railway warehouse into a hospital for 5,000 men administered by thirty doctors and nurses. Since the railroad had been destroyed, large scale and rapid evacuation to the rear was out of the question. In "that pitiful shed of horrors" wounded Anglo-Americans begged for water and morphine while Russian tankers were promptly transported to Barcelona by air.[1]

Steve Nelson was wounded at Belchite and was treated at the field hospital at La Puebla de Hijar at the same time Sam was. He described the horror of the hospital ward in *The Volunteers*. For all we know, Sam was one of the nameless boys who cried out while Steve Nelson was there.

---

1. Eby, *Comrades and Commissars*, 256.

STEVE NELSON

White Sheets

"Where am I?" I looked around the large, poorly lit room. My lips were parched and my tongue felt as dry as old shoe leather. Everything smelled of ether. A man groaned and called for help.

I looked up and saw a long line of low metal beds, at least 50, and full of wounded. I heard a faint sound of artillery fire. I concluded that I was in a field hospital not far from the front. I knew of only one hospital near the front. It was reserved for head and abdominal cases. Others had to be taken further to the rear. What was I doing here?

As far as I knew I had not been seriously wounded. Perhaps I had been hit on the way to the hospital. I got frightened at the thought. My hands involuntarily reached under the sheet feeling myself. Then I remembered, I had been brought to this hospital by Dr. Strauss. All the ambulances were gone at the time.

The cries of the wounded were louder and more numerous. I sat up, leaning against the cold metal bedstead, looking at the two long lines of wounded in the ward. There was no sign of life in several of them. The sheets were drawn over patients' faces in several of them. I counted nine beds motionless, the dark blankets removed. I realized that all those were dead. I noted that they weren't even taken out of the ward. Just covered with a white sheet.

A nurse came rushing by, and I inquired, "Are there any Americans here?" "Oh, yes," she said, "*mucho, mucho Americano,*" pointing to the end of the room.

Several men were just brought in, still on stretchers. Their bandages drenched with blood.

I strained my eyes towards the door, and recognized the large man on the stretcher as "Charlie the Sniper."

Charlie gave me a knowing glance and said, "I'm hit, but I will be all right." He raised the bloody bandaged stump of his left arm. "This is where I got it." Raising himself slightly on the stretcher, he said, "But, I still got this one," raising his right hand, and closing it into a fist.

I raised mine. Charlie slumped on the pillow. His arm dropped heavily on the side of the stretcher to the floor. The nurse motioned to a doctor to come to Charlie's stretcher. They worked on him for a while, but did not attempt to take off his clothes, not to move him from the corridor into the ward. I worried and thought that things were going bad with the "Sniper." The doctor looked around and slowly pulled the white sheet towards Charlie's face. I was sitting up looking at what was going on, and when the doctor took the white sheet he suddenly turned to avoid looking at Charlie's dead body.

Three beds from me a man began to moan. He said something unintelligible but the voice sounded familiar. I reared up. To my astonishment, I saw Paul Block, the company political commissar who helped to carry me when I was hit a short while ago. Paul's eyes opened but he did not recognize me. He was sweating and struggling for breath. The nurse and the doctor came, took his pulse and began to work on him. With a worried look, the doctor said, "An oxygen tent is what we need, but we haven't got one." Paul recovered consciousness for a short while, recognized me. He asked for water, "Water, Steve." He grasped my hand, and even while unconscious, he held me tight. He gasped, his hand loosening its hold. He did not recover consciousness. He was covered like the other ten.

What I saw here was worse than anything I ever experienced. The passing of comrades was hard to take. Men were killed at the front, but it never had this effect on me. I realized why. In action at the very time of death, the fight has to go on, but out of action it was different. Lying in a hospital seeing men suffer and die like flies was frightening. I tried to turn my mind from the dead comrades, but the more I tried, the more vividly I saw them in life.[2]

2. Nelson, *The Volunteers*, 188.

16

September 1937

In Case of Death

SAM

SUPPOSE I do get bumped off. Suppose Harry won't write home for me like he's promised. I better do it myself. But suppose I'm just wounded. Suppose some fool finds the letters to Mother and Clara and sends 'em off. Nice anticlimax! But I've got to risk it.

It's harder to write than I'd thought. Somehow I keep thinking of that book at home, *Letters of Fallen Englishmen*. Too bad I can't just say, "Dear Parents, Consult *Letters of Fallen Englishmen*. Most of those boys were young like me, just past twenty; most of them loved their parents. Same sentiments here." But of course that won't do . . .

LOVE AND REVOLUTIONARY GREETINGS

In Case of death only, please send
this to Mrs. Lee J. Levinger, 2257
Indianola Ave., Columbus, Ohio, U.
S. A. Do not send in case of in-
jury. Thanks, comrade.
Samuel Levinger

Dear Mother and Father:

I suppose that by the time you receive this, I will have been dead several weeks. Of course, war is a confused thing, and I have seen enough certified corpses walking around to make me a little sceptical, but if you receive this and an official announcement too, count it as definite.

This is the last day of relief. We are going up to some front tomorrow to clear out the Fascists. I do not doubt that we will be successful in repatriating the boys across the street, but it will be at considerable cost, and as the Lincoln Battalion is good it should be in the middle of it.

I still stick by my original conviction that I will be alive long after a whole lot of dictators have died of lead poisoning or hardened arteries; but I have been wrong on other matters before. Hence I decided to write this letter.

Certainly I am not enthusiastic about dying. I have gotten a good bit of fun out of my first twenty years despite the fact that, except for the last six months, they were pretty useless. I suppose I would have enjoyed my next twenty just as much. I wanted to write this letter, however, to make clear that there is absolutely nothing to regret.

If I were alive again I think I would join in the battle again at this crucial place. There was an extremely important job to do over here and I was one of the men who decided to do it. That a good many of us were killed while doing it is unfortunate, and the fact that I was killed is still more unfortunate from our standpoints. However, this has no relevance to the necessity of doing the job. The difference between world Fascism and world socialism is far too great to permit our safeties to be a factor for consideration.

Next I want to beg both of you not to see this out of context. World change is a stern master. It had killed and will kill millions of boys as dear to somebody as I am to you. The Fascists want war, and bitter war we will give them.

You are more fortunate than many of the parents, for you still have two children with extremely bright futures. You have your extremely valuable work. I am less able to evaluate Father's work, though I realise its great worth; but in my field, that of an author, I can say I think Mother should become one of the most valuable authors of the generation. And you still have the emancipation of America to be achieved.

I think my ideas on immortality agree largely with yours. I once wrote a lousy poem "If there is darkness beyond I shall sleep, if light I shall wake." So if I meet you folks again all to the good-- if not, we've had quite a bit of pleasure in each other's company while it lasted.

As for my friends, give them my love if you run across them. Tell them I said there's only one thing to remember--that there's one comrade less to do the job of soldier of discontent. They'll all have to do some work to make up for my getting perforated. See if that will get a few of these mugwumps into action.

This has been a clumsy letter. I just want to say that I love you both a great deal, and so forth. Also that it isn't such a serious thing.

Love and revolutionary greetings.

Joy to the world.

Samuel Levinger

Aug or Sept 1937

* To read the full text of this letter refer to the Appendix.

It was even harder to write to Clara, but I knew I'd better do it now that I had my steam up. And I'm sure that Mother will show Clara the longer letter, too. It's nice to know that Clara is staying with Father and Mother now and intends to be with them until she got through college—it would make it nicer for everybody. But—I'm getting tired—I better get on with writing this letter.

> Dear Clara,
> Just a word to tell you not to take this thing too hard . . . You'll have lots of trouble in your life, and here's a little more. To some extent however that's the case with the whole of our generation. Capitalism demands its victims, and we got hit a trifle worse than most. The main point is that we're hitting back. I just wanted to write a note to tell you that I loved you a Hell of a lot. It would have been very good to have been with you always. But since it didn't work out that way we'll have to carry on differently. Remember I loved you very deeply. I'm not sorry I came. I think I contributed a little to the fight over here. I know your life will be full of action and accomplishment—I think it will be full of joy, too.
> Love. *Salud*. Joy to the World.

I grinned over the last line—though it wasn't really that funny—I'm a fine one to be writing Joy to the World to a girl I'll probably never kiss again.[1]

1. Private collection.

17

September 5, 1937

Final Hours

SAM

PLENTY HAPPENING now in Belchite although I knew there wasn't much I could do about it. Plenty of time to think, too, when the pain lets you. Morphia helped but it gets you drowsy and you know you mustn't go to sleep. You have more important things to do—like writing letters.

They must have been surprised back at the other hospital when they found me and my clothes gone; but they ought to be used to it, with so many of the fellows deserting back to the lines as soon as they could walk. Too bad I missed Quinto! Must have been a hell of a good fight. And just my luck to run into Amalie here at Belchite. He said: "I thought you were going home." I said: "Yes, sir, but everybody says this is going to be such a lovely battle."

Smith didn't argue with me neither. When he saw me get off the truck that picked me up down the road he just said: "So you're back, are you? Isn't that fine? You know considerable Spanish. Want to do a little scouting for me?" So I did. Got close enough to hear 'em talking. Smith liked my report. Then he told me to take a machine gun and have somebody help me carry it if I felt too weak. Have to write a note to the kids to tell 'em where I dropped it when

I got knocked out. Wonder if they got that church by now? Like to ask Smith but he looks like he's sleeping; don't want to bother him.

Nice guy, Smith. Brought up to be a preacher. Says he's got a real religion now. Wonder if that's his real name. He keeps joking, saying it's no use to change his name like so many of the fellows have, 'cause Smith is enough of an alibi. Wonder whether he'll pull through; got his right through the chest. More dignified than me. Like me to take my shrapnel through the guts.

Have to tell 'em at home it's a leg wound, like all the fellows do. Don't worry the women so—no disfigurement. Not like coming home shell-shocked or blind. Mother always fussing when we were kids—put each other's eyes out if we didn't stop having mud-fights or playing with the clothes poles in the backyard. Did knock Kiddo's front tooth out; called him Cowface for years.

Now a blood transfusion. Wish they'd let me alone. "Oh that's all right, Miss Silverstine, I'm pretty comfortable. Mother and baby doing fine! You know my mother had to go to the hospital once for an operation when we three kids were little, and before she went, she said to us: 'If any one of you goes around to the neighbors saying I went to the hospital to get a baby, I'll scalp you.' Say, you're busy and I'm keeping you here talking. What would I like? Say, I'd give a dollar if I had it just for a glass of fresh milk instead of this canned stuff. You're going to try to get me some? Thanks a lot."

The next morning my right leg was put in traction and they were putting a tube in me to drain my bladder. That hurt. I hoped I didn't make too much fuss. Always was a fool about pain. When we were all kids and had to get vaccinated or to get shots before going abroad, Kiddo and Leah always had to go first to show me it didn't hurt. Guess that's why I admired Jesus so much; stood his pain all that time and then didn't swear at the bastards who were torturing him. Myrtle said so. Myrtle used to look the other way when I stole her cookies!

Think of something else so it won't hurt so much. That little monument sort of we put up for the men who died at Jarama. Hung a helmet on it. Walter told me I should write something for the board. Thought I was quite a kid 'cause I wrote things for our wall newspaper. What in hell did I say? Oh yes: "To Our Fallen Comrades—Our Victory is your Vengeance." Not bad, not at all bad.

"Yes, I've got enough paper, Miss Silverstine. But this pencil keeps breaking. Maybe, I press down too hard. No, I don't need you to write it, thanks. I know how busy you are."

"Dear Mother," I began, *but why is the pencil so heavy?* "I'm now in the hospital with a nice safe little wound. The bullet missed the bone on the right leg, then missed the bone on the left." That'll make 'em all feel better. "Should be all rested in a month; although Comrade Amalie, the Battalion Commander, says I've done my share at the front. Would you advise me to take a truck driver job or to go home? I'm writing you just how I promised—if there was anything serious I should inform you. I can't write for a little while because I'm short of paper." *If I ever get through this . . .* "I hope your ivy poisoning is okay.

In Jarama I wrote an extremely sentimental note to be sent in case of death. I lost it since. So if a philosophical note turns up deploring my death, think nothing of it. I seem to be out of the front for good. Love to Everybody."

ELMA

I imagined it must have been something like this:

A boy who knew, Leah, Sam's sister in New York, came hobbling down the harrow aisle between the beds. Lucky bastard, he's really shot in the leg. No damn tube in the guts for him: Want a cigarette, Sam? Nurse Silverstine's lips began to form a "No." Then she nodded. The boy from New York caught the death sentence. Then, he guessed, it didn't matter if he tired Sam out by talking.

He'd meant to ask him for messages for Leah to give the folks back home. But now, his note finished, Sam wanted to talk only of the work that remained to be done back in America. Yes, he'd have plenty to write about now . . . And he wanted to go into union work. Unions were the hope of America. If they'd only see what Fascism had done to them—was going to do to 'em—well, it would be hard to keep a Union man out of Spain . . ."I always carried my card with me in my billfold . . . but I lost it . . . there were letters . . ."

Miss Silverstine drove the boy from New York away. Sam wished he didn't feel so sleepy. Anyhow, he'd finished his letter. "Not to be delivered except in case of death." He was too tired now. Anyhow, his pencil had broken again. Cheap pencils always did.

He remembered Mrs. Sellers, that woman who always looked tired and walked like an old woman although she was younger than Mother. He remembered her in the dusk on the porch with the least kid on her lap, like she called him, singing, "Rock me to sleep, Mother, rock me to sleep."

His head swayed from side to side. Nice to be rocked again. Like floating down the river in a canoe, the waves slapping at the sides. "Rock me to sleep."

The ragged young orderly went on mopping the tiled floor. Swish—swish—waves—swish.

The bandages must have soaked through again—he didn't want to bother that nice nurse who looked ready to drop, but if he told her he was wet and messy—a hell of a place to get shot— like that fellow in the Hemingway story—no kids now, never— but maybe a man who was going to spend his life hustling for the working class was just as well off–nice to hear those waves— swish—swish—. He'd have to get up and change his pajamas; put these to the wash before Mother found 'em when she'd make the bed . . . But it was pleasant to lie there drifting, drifting, back to his first watery home in the dark womb. Drifting.

The ragged orderly scowled. Those stretcher-bearers were careless and it would take a lot of water before those red blotches faded. He brought two large pails and poured a heavy stream.

Sam tried to lift his head. Why, he wasn't back in his bed at home! He'd climbed his first mountain, fried his supper of fish, and wrapped himself in his poncho for the night. Nice little mountain stream! His hands gripped the sheets. The orderly had seen many men die during the last few days; he waited dully.

Sleeping in the mountains, beside a stream that fell sheer and sharply to the rocks below. There'd been a battle in the mountains. He'd have to ask Smith about it. But he couldn't see Smith any more. And what was Smith doing in the mountains, anyhow . . .

Smith awoke just as the orderly pulled up the sheet on the next bed. He wondered afterwards if it was because he was so weak himself that he turned his face to the wall and cried.[1]

1. E. Levinger, *Death in the Mountains*, 173.

18

1937–1998

Remembering Sam

ELMA

RALPH BATES, who knew him well over there, told us many stories of his jokes, his never-failing good spirits, and the determination which make a boy always awkward with his hands into a crack machine-gunner. Just the other day a message came from a boy still in Spain who was with him in hospital for the last five hours before his death. This boy wrote, "Those five hours will mean more to me that anything that ever happened to me before or may ever happen again in all my life."

And then in early December we received this letter from Rubin Ryant, one of Sam's comrades. It meant the world to us.

> November 15, 1937
> Albacete, Spain

Dear Mr. Levinger,

Having fought in the machine gun company of the Lincoln Battalion alongside of Samuel for the entire length of time that he was with us, it was only natural that Bill Lawrence should ask me to tell you about Sam.

LOVE AND REVOLUTIONARY GREETINGS

My first acquaintance with Sam was in the early days of February at Jarama when the fascist war machine was trying to capture the Madrid-Valencia Highway. At that time our machine gun company was of little importance as a machine gun unit. Thanks to the policy of "non-intervention" our guns were just so much scrap iron. Period. So we used rifles instead. And it was on the firing line alongside of me with a smoking rifle in his hands and a big grin on his face that I met Sam. He seemed to be getting quite a kick out of the fierce fighting.

A couple of days later we organized a food, water and ammunition detail to get the stuff up to the front line. Sam was one of the first to volunteer for the job. And it was hard, dangerous nerve wracking work because the men were under fire practically the whole time. Still that was typical of Sam.

He would always volunteer for the hard, dangerous task. Always with a big friendly grin on his face. And if he had anything to share with the boys he would do so without hesitation. He lent me his poncho one cold, wet miserable night in early March. I'm sure I would have frozen stiff without it.

As time passed and we all settled into the routine of life in the trenches, Sam kept working hard. Whenever there was any fighting to be done, he would grab a rifle and run into the trenches. When things were quiet he would try to outdo all the other comrades in digging trenches, building machine gun emplacements and digging dugouts. At the same time he kept perfecting his ability as a machine gunner until he was a really good gunner.

Several times I'd kid him about working so hard and he would invariably answer that there was a war going on. It seemed to me that there was something just driving him on, never permitting him to rest. He seemed as though he could never do enough, when there was so much to do.

The fascists must be defeated and by working and fighting still harder our victory would be nearer by that much.

On April 5th we attacked the fascists at Jarama. The fascists laid down a heavy barrage of both heavy artillery and shrapnel between our front line and the ammunition dump. Sam outdid himself that day making trip after trip through that curtain of fire for machine gun ammunition. He was the moving spirit of the entire ammo detail.

During the Brunete offensive he was assistant battalion armorer. He was slightly wounded by some pieces of rock that hit him during a plane bombardment. Instead of staying in the hospital until he was entirely well, he ran away from there in order to rejoin the battalion. There was no holding him back. That burning, fighting hatred of fascism that kept driving him forward brought him to his death.

At Belchite during the Aragon offensive it was necessary to take the church at the edge of the town. It was the highest point of the town, well fortified and commanding the headquarters of the fascist garrison. The assault on the church was made by a number of groups of men attacking from different points. Sam led one of these groups. Despite the fact that he was not supposed to be there. He should have stayed by the ammunition dump which was a reasonably safe position. Instead, he put a reliable comrade in charge and ran up to the front lines to take part in the attack.

A fascist machine gun cut him down as he was leading his men.

He was a good friend of mine and his death leaves me with a feeling of deep personal loss. And the working class suffered a deep loss, for he was a good comrade, a brave fighter and a real hero in every sense of the word.

Please accept my sincere condolences.

Comradely yours,

Rubin Ryant

LOVE AND REVOLUTIONARY GREETINGS

RABBI LEE LEVINGER, 1938

Dear Mr. White,

It gives me great regret that I cannot arrange to be with you for the meeting of the Veterans of December 11.

Samuel was one of you, devoted to the same cause for which you have all served and sacrificed, and his family are enlisted for life in the same service on the home front.

I know as a veteran of the World War how much a veterans' organization can mean, not only for the very important task of keeping together the men who have such deep common interests and experiences, but even more in lining them up for a common platform for the future. The cause of anti-fascism alone is one which will undoubtedly call for continued action in the future, and it is one where your experiences will make you doubly useful in America. And there are certainly other principles and other realizations of yours which will become a part of your continuing platform.

Give my best wishes to the new organization and the men who are establishing it.

Very sincerely,
Rabbi Lee Levinger
National Chaplain, The American Legion

Sarah Lawrence, the college where Leah was a sophomore, did their part.

> THE CAMPUS, March 1938
> Loyalist Ambulance Attracts Attention
>   on S. L. Campus
> Tin-Foil Aids In Purchase Of $1,000 Supply Carrier

Anyone looking out on Westlands driveway last Wednesday afternoon around 3:00 would not have noticed anything very different or exciting. There were the same black shiny town cars in which sat liveried chauffeurs, a few open roadsters and two or three girls in regular polo coats. Suddenly, something happened that changed the whole scene, something that will probably never happen again to Westlands driveway. A long blue car drove in as quietly and inconspicuously as possible. It drove in and parked in one of the empty spaces. Someone realized that at last the ambulance which had been talked of for so long had arrived. Pretty soon girls had gathered around looking at the car and talking to the driver.

On the door of the car was written the names of colleges that had donated money to purchase it. There were seven of these including a Faculty Committee. The only symbol on the car was a red cross painted on a white circle.

The driver turned out to be an attractive young man who said he had tried to get into the Spanish Loyalist Army for a year.

"They are not taking any more volunteers from this country so I have to spend my time touring the United States trying to get funds for the Medical Bureau to Aid Spanish Democracy," he said.

This, by the way, is the bureau that has benefited from money received for tinfoil that has been sold back to tinfoil manufacturers. A. S. U. members handed the driver the twenty odd pounds of tinfoil they have been collecting from cigarette packages since last October.

The car which cost $1,000 will be shipped to Spain on the 30th of this month. The girls were surprised to find out that what they were observing was really not an ambulance but a medical supply carrier, which could be used as an ambulance by putting in two stretchers.

"You might be wondering why the car is blue instead of white," the driver explained, "it is much harder to see the blue and the white is so conspicuous it can be bombed easily. For instance, the Harvard ambulance that is painted white has already been bombarded three times."

While watching the car drive out of the Sarah Lawrence driveway one was lost in a world of time and space, when realizing that that same car would soon be on a battle torn field in a distant country.[1]

LEAH, 1950

The year before he went to Spain my brother Sam was in the seamen's union; he came to see Genevieve Taggard, one of my professors, with me in her home once or twice and they liked each other immensely. Then, when he went to Spain, she was one of the first people I told, and showed her some of his letters. We talked about the Spanish often, for it was the front line of our battle, but since she knew and liked Sam as a person I could talk more with her just about him. Then when he died she and another friend of mine brought me the news, and it wasn't a time where political perspective could matter at all. She cried for him. It was a long time until I was able to cry myself, and to face losing someone I loved as a stark human tragedy without its political rationalizations. Genevieve's crying on that day helped me to do this. The many days afterwards when I saw her, often we didn't talk about him, but about my school work, or student activities, fund raising for Spain, or other things, but always my knowing how much she cared too about the death of one individual. What she helped teach me about suffering is all of a piece with what she helped me learn about poetry; neither grief nor art are to be taken in one's stride, labeled, understood, put in the appropriate mental compartment; they are real and must be experienced uncritically and whole-heartedly if one is to grow as a human being.[2]

1. Private collection.
2. Private collection.

LEAH, 1974

Both Elma and Lee trembled for Sam's safety as he was still so young, but with their belief in independence they felt he should do what he chose. Besides trembling for his safety it was often a considerable degree of embarrassment for them as the papers would play up with a large headline "Rabbi's Son On Chain Gang," etc. But they really encouraged him a good deal, both because they themselves felt that there was no simple answer to how one should deal with the ills of our day and while they themselves were tremendously hard workers on committees and writing and petitions, etc., Sam's more active methods might be the answer. Then came Spain and this was a particularly hard thing for each of them to accept. Lee had been, ever since his experience in World War I, an ardent pacifist and believed that he had raised us children with the same convictions. Yet here, too, with his feeling about Hitler and Mussolini and fascism in general, he understood Sam's need to go and fight for the Spanish Republic. Elma had somewhat shared these views and probably was even more in anguish about Sam going for he was so close to her. The two of them looked alike and he had very much her social qualities of winning everybody whom he met. Indeed years after his death various odd characters would appear at the house and say that Sammy had told them that if they were ever in Columbus to go and see his mother and she would give them a meal. Sam went to Spain in January of 1937 and the news of his death, which actually occurred in September, reached the family in October 1937. During those ten months and afterwards until the defeat of the Spanish Republic, both Lee and Elma made working for Spain their major activity . . . After Sam's death a memorial meeting was held in New York for him as a way of raising money for an ambulance. It was too painful for Elma to travel at that point but Lee went to the meeting and quietly endured hearing all the eulogies. Something probably went out of their life with the death of this oldest son. Elma survived him for almost twenty years and Lee for thirty and they made many new friends, traveled much, Elma wrote her most successful books afterwards and they took great pride in the careers of their remaining children. But time and again when one of the other spoke of Sam it would be with a sense of irreparable loss.[3]

UNKNOWN

To the International Battalion
In memory of a young American, just turned twenty, who was a "soldier for liberty" in Spain.

You are the seed of tomorrow.
From your corpse rotting in the acrid soil of Spain
Will grow an olive tree.
Its deep roots watered by your blood;
Its revolt-twisted trunk drawing strength from your flesh,
To branch into clear air
And blossom star-white on the future horizon,
In the green springtime of freedom
And the warm glow of peace.
But the olives will burn blood red in the autumn
When the storm and the whirlwind come,
Burn red as your quick blood.
And the firm fleshed young fruit
Too soon fallen, will rot purpling the ground;
Making rich soil for liberty.[4]

LEON SLAVIN, 1989

Another's Word

In memory of Sam Levinger,
killed in Spain, 1937, fighting fascists.

3. Private collection.
4. Private collection.

I said to him; don't go to Spain.
And so we argued on—
Of Stalin's purges—were they bad?
And what of Trotsky—was he mad?
Till half the night was done.

He went to war and ne'er returned.
His girlfriend pale with strain,
Laughed mockingly that he had said
The theories that I'd advance
Had not improved, when heard in Spain.

I smiled politely, turned my head;
I would not quarrel with the dead.

Yet there was more, I knew e'en then.
The argument that we had had—
The words, the phrases, the clichés—
They all had come from other men.
I'd really meant: You're not eighteen.
Why seek out battles? They'll arrive!
Your girlfriend's here.
We are your friends.
Remain with us! Remain alive!

These words I felt were never heard,
Immured too deep behind a wall
From which at times I would emerge
Riding a war horse all my own
And armed with another's word.[5]

LOUIS BROMFIELD
American author and conservationist,
1927 Pulitzer Prize winner

This is the story of a hero in the best American sense,
of a boy who gave his life that liberty might endure at a

5. Private Collection.

moment when opportunists, politicians, greedy industrialists and even dignitaries of the church in Europe and
American were doing their best to throttle and destroy
it. They succeeded for a little while but their materialistic
opportunist victory was an ironic one in which lay the
very seeds of their destruction. Those shameful elements
from the odious Father Coughlin in Detroit to the evil
Sir John Simon in the midst of the appeasing oligarchy
in Whitehall, worked and intrigued and propagandized
as allies of Hitler and Mussolini until the First Spanish
Republic was at last overwhelmed by a curious and mal-
odorous alliance of Medievalism, Industrial Capitalism
and Nazism. I say overwhelmed and not conquered because the Spanish Republic is certain to rise again one day
since humanity cannot and must not return to the dark
ages. Out of the sinister defeat of the Spanish Republic
came the monstrous war in which the same elements
which opposed the Republic are again allied in a dark and
sinister confusion founded upon an indecent self-interest
and materialism—the appeasers, the old speculators, the
Fifth columnists, the manufacturers who hate their own
workmen, the churchmen who seek to thrust mankind
back into that epoch where it becomes once more a victim
of a politically ambitious church. Against the background
of these figures, the figure of the boy in this story shines
bright and heroic as an American of Americans, in the
pure and best tradition of a nation which has written
into its constitution its belief in liberty, decency and human dignity. He was, as every true son of the New World
Republic should be–adventurous, curious, a little fanatic,
and given to action as well as thought. He was one of the
many American boys who went to Spain believing that
human liberty was the thing in all the world most worth
fighting for.

I know a great many of these boys and young men who left homes in countries all over the world to go to Spain and fight in behalf of the Republic against the Unholy Alliance. Many of them were killed—many were returned home at last wounded, ill and blind, with hearts broken but spirits undefeated.

As one of the Committee for American Wounded from Spain, I helped to repatriate them when the collapse finally came, and even to do this—to battle endlessly with the dark forces of the Unholy Alliance. But out of the struggle which culminated in triumph and success, there emerged many things which made the hard work and the disgust and heartbreak seem light indeed. Individuals in the government and elsewhere revealed nobility of thought and action. Rich men showed themselves amazingly and unexpectedly generous. People without means worked themselves ill to help. The Spanish debacle brought together in common sympathy a kind of aristocracy of spirit and generosity. But greatest of all experiences was that of knowing the young men like Sam Levinger who heard the call of Liberty in distress and answered it.

The story of the International Brigade in Spain is one of the great stories of history. Ernest Hemingway, who lived side by side with these volunteers, has written some of it. One day it will be written in full, with all its beauty and heroism and splendor with due consideration, I hope, of the dark and evil forces which fought these idealists.

Sam Levinger was one of the Brigade. His story is that of an exceptionally imaginative, gifted American boy brought up in a family which lived more in spirit than in the bank vault. He was the spiritual descendant of the undefeatable revolutionists of 1776, of the Abolitionists and the men who helped the slaves to escape through his own state of Ohio northward to the freedom of Canada.

His story is told here, partly in his own writing and partly by his mother, herself an heroic woman devoted to the Cause of Humanity. I commend it to you with the hope that there will be more and more Americans like Sam Levinger.[6]

MURRAY KEMPTON
American Journalist, 1985 Pulitzer Prize winner

There has been a radical in America whose tradition was defeat and whose end was community. His was a voice almost stilled among the radicals of the thirties; and now, at a time when the radicals of the thirties have been driven to cover or recantation of dreadful isolation, we listen for his voice again. He was the radical who dared to stand alone, to whom no man called out in vain, to whom the lie was dishonorable and the crawl degrading . . . I think of him as perhaps like Sam Levinger, who is dead in a grave which is either unmarked or desecrated in Franco's Spain and who wrote before he died:

> Comrades, the battle is bloody and the war is long,
> Still let us climb the gray hills and charge the guns.

Those are tired words, and they have absorbed all the agony which is the truth of life. They are resigned, but they are undefeated. They do not suggest that somebody else charge the guns. They know the worst, but they will make the charge themselves. I miss them very much and I wish we had them back."[7]

6. Private Collection.
7. Kempton, *Part of Our Time*, 333–34.

STAUGHTON LYND
Peace activist, historian, author, lawyer

When I was five- or six-years old, a young man named Sam Levinger carried me on his shoulders in a May Day parade in New York City. Later that year Sam Levinger went to Spain as a volunteer for the Abraham Lincoln Brigade. As a child I was told that he was wounded in the groin by machine gun fire, and died because the medical supplies were inadequate. Recently I was asked to review a book on the Abraham Lincoln Brigade, and learned more facts about Sam Levinger. He came from Columbus and attended Ohio State. His father was a rabbi. For the last sixty years I have assumed that Sam Levinger was a Communist, as were most of the volunteers for the Lincoln Brigade. Now I learn that he was a member of the Young Peoples Socialist League, as I might have been had I been fifteen years older. I learned the date and place he was fatally wounded: in September 1937, at Belchite. These facts are all new to me, but the inward, essential meaning of Sam Levinger's life and death became part of me as a child. I do not even actually remember being carried on his shoulders. Like so much of oral history, it was told to me, and I accepted it as true, and it was true. Levinger touched my life, teaching me without words that one should be prepared to give one's all for an ideal.

19

Barcelona, November 1, 1938

The International Brigade Leaves Spain

LA PASIONARIA, DOLORES IBARRURI
Spanish Republican leader

IT IS very difficult to say a few words in farewell to the heroes of the International Brigades, because of what they are, what they represent. A feeling of sorrow, an infinite grief catches our throat—sorrow for those who are going away, for the soldiers of the highest ideal of human redemption, exiles from their countries, persecuted by the tyrants of all peoples—grief for those who will stay here forever mingled with the Spanish soil, in the very depth of our heart, hallowed by our feeling of eternal gratitude.

From all peoples, from all races, you came to us like brothers, like sons of immortal Spain; and in the hardest days of the war, when the capital of the Spanish Republic was threatened, it was you, gallant comrades of the International Brigades, who helped save the city with your fighting enthusiasm, your heroism and your spirit of sacrifice. —And Jarama and Guadalajara, Brunete and Belchite, Levante and the Ebro, in immortal verses sing of the courage, the sacrifice, the daring, and the discipline of the men of the International Brigades.

For the first time in the history of the peoples' struggles, there was the spectacle, breathtaking in its grandeur, of the formation of the International Brigades to help save a threatened country's freedom and independence—the freedom and independence of our Spanish land.

Communists, Socialists, Anarchists, Republicans—men of different colors, differing ideology, antagonistic religions—yet all profoundly loving liberty and justice, they came and offered themselves to us unconditionally.

They gave us everything—their youth or their maturity; their science or their experience; their blood and their lives; their hopes and aspirations—and they asked us for nothing. But yet, it must be said, they did want a post in battle, they aspired to the honor of dying for us.

Banners of Spain! Salute these many heroes! Be lowered to honor so many martyrs!

Mothers! Women! When the years pass by and the wounds of war are stanched; when the memory of the sad and bloody days dissipates in a present of liberty, of peace and of wellbeing; when the rancors have died out and pride in a free country is felt equally by all Spaniards, speak to your children. Tell them of these men of the International Brigades.

Recount for them how, coming over seas and mountains, crossing frontiers bristling with bayonets, sought by raving dogs thirsting to tear their flesh, these men reached our country as crusaders for freedom, to fight and die for Spain's liberty and independence threatened by German and Italian fascism. They gave up everything—their loves, their countries, home and fortune, fathers, mothers, wives, brothers, sisters and children—and they came and said to us: "We are here. Your cause, Spain's cause, is ours. It is the cause of all advanced and progressive mankind."

Today many are departing. Thousands remain, shrouded in Spanish earth, profoundly remembered by all Spaniards. Comrades of the International Brigades: Political reasons, reasons of state, the welfare of that very cause for which you offered your blood with boundless generosity, are sending you back, some to your own countries and others to forced exile. You can go proudly. You are history. You are legend. You are the heroic example of democracy's solidarity and universality in the face of the vile and accommodating spirit of those who interpret democratic principles with their eyes on hoards of wealth or corporate shares which they want to safeguard from all risk.

We shall not forget you; and, when the olive tree of peace is in flower, entwined with the victory laurels of the Republic of Spain—come back!

Come back to us. To our side for here you will find a homeland—those who have no country or friends, who must live deprived of friendship—all, all will have the affection and gratitude of the Spanish people who today and tomorrow will shout with enthusiasm—.

Long live the heroes of the International Brigades![1]

1. Osheroff and Susman, *No Pasarán!*, 18.

20

The Brigade Comes Home

WHAT WELCOME did the surviving members of the Lincoln Brigade receive when they returned to the United States?

Time Magazine, January 2, 1939

> National Affairs: Boys from Brunete
> - When 1,500,000 U.S. boys came back from France in 1919, the bands played "Over There", "K-K-K-Katy", "The Star Spangled Banner", and crowds lionized them.
> - When 322 U.S. boys and a girl came back from Spain last week, a small crowd did the lionizing, and the song was again "The Star-Spangled Banner".
>
> They were fighters in a war in which the U. S. is neutral, veterans of the Abraham Lincoln Brigade, organized in January 1937 to fight for Loyalist Spain. The brigade mustered altogether 4,000 U. S. citizens. Last September the Spanish Leftist Government disbanded it. Those who filed last week from the third-class gangplanks of the Cunarder Ausonia to a Manhattan dock had left behind some 2,000 killed and missing, 250 captured at Belchite, Brunete, many another battleground. (Others are still in Spain or convalescing in France, and 870 veterans had already returned to the U.S.)
>
> Typical of the brigade's personnel was the roll of last week's homecomers. Among them: 25-year-old Brigade Commissar (political instructor) John Gates from Youngstown, Ohio; Sergeant Gerald Cook, office boy for the pinko *Nation*; Lieut. Manny Lancer, formerly of the Workers Alliance; Sergeant

Thomas Page, a Manhattan Negro (wounded on the Ebro front): an Iowan who became Captain Owen Smith; 20-year-old Nurse Rose Waxman of Manhattan. Saddest of the heroes was a lad whose parents met him at the dock, snatched off his purple military beret, hopped up & down on it, indignantly marched him home.

As the most active defender of Loyalist Spain in the U.S., the Communist Party had a big hand in recruiting the brigade, slipping its rookies into Spain and naming the outfit (for Abraham Lincoln is now a Communist hero by adoption).

21

The War Before the Lights Went Out

DOROTHY PARKER
American poet and satirist

I N THE introduction to *The Heart of Spain*, an anthology of fiction, nonfiction, and poetry about the Spanish Civil War, Dorothy Parker writes:

> I stayed in Valencia and in Madrid, places I had not been since that fool of a king lounged on the throne, and in those two cities and in the country around and between them, I met the best people anyone ever knew. I had never seen such people before. But I shall see their like again. And so shall all of us. If I did not believe that, I think I should stand up in front of my mirror and take a long, deep swinging slash at my throat.
>
> For what they stood for, what they have given others to take and hold and carry along–it does not vanish from the earth. This is not a matter of wishing or feeling; it is knowing. It is knowing that nothing devised by fat, rich, frightened men can ever stamp out truth and courage, and determination for a decent life.
>
> It is impossible not to feel sad for what happened to the Loyalists in Spain; heaven grant we will never not be sad at stupidity and greed. To be sorry for those people—no. It is a shameful, strutting impudence to be sorry for the noble. But there is no shame to honorable anger, the anger that comes

and stays against those who saw and would not aid, those who looked and shrugged and turned away.[1]

HELEN GRAHAM
British historian and author

The Spanish Civil War was, in a sense, the war before the lights went out—the war that could have changed the course of European and world history if power actors had behaved in different ways. And it was such a transformational site, culturally, for so many different kinds of people, that Spain was a magic territory . . .[2]

Denunciation was a major mechanism to trigger the detention and trial of Republicans in post-war Spain. But priests were not the only denouncers. Tens of thousands of ordinary Spaniards also responded to the regime's enthusiastic encouragement—out of political conviction, social prejudice, opportunism, or fear. They denounced their neighbors, acquaintances, and even family members—denunciations for which no corroboration was either sought or required. Even though the system itself was instigated by the regime, the consequences of denunciation created dense webs of complicity and collaboration. In other words, the work of legitimating Francoism and building its brutal community was occurring deep inside Spanish society.[3]

ABEL PLENN
American journalist and author

Civil War in Spain has never stopped since 1936 when it was first provoked by Franco and his Axis-supported army. Bloodletting has been and continues to be the order of the day under the Franco terror. The state of unrest in Spain is

1. In Bessie, ed., *Heart of Spain*, introduction.
2. Faber and Fernandez, "War Before the Lights Went Out," 4.
3. Graham, *The Spanish Civil War*, 135.

growing worse because the Spanish people—through their spreading resistance movement and the moral encouragement offered by those countries which, unlike us, have broken or are preparing to break off relations with fascist Spain–now look forward more confidently to the day when Franco and his fascist collaborators will be swept from power.[4]

A SPANISH CHILD REFUGEE

A war is when troops rush in the streets and father went away and didn't come back and bombs fell and mother died and we have nothing to eat and brother went out too and said he was going to meet father and he didn't come back. And Aunt Catherine and I were put on a train and brought here where we don't know anyone and can't speak and are alone.[5]

4. Plenn, *Wind in the Olive Trees*, 338.
5. Barsky and Waugh, "The Surgeon Goes to War," 237.

22

How We Begin to Remember

This is the powerful pulsing of love in the veins[1]

LAURIE

SAM'S PHOTOGRAPH hung on the wall in every house where I've lived. I remember him from when I was a child, and, when we asked, my father told us his name, but nothing more. It was obvious to all of us that we must not ask questions. Sam was a mystery, ever-present, but silent. When I moved to my own home and had my own children, I tried to fill in some of the blanks of the story of the boy-soldier-turned-hero who died in Spain when he was twenty.

This story, like most of mine, takes a circuitous route, following twists and detours, over and through, before arriving somewhere. Somewhere that means something, makes some kind of sense, so that you look back and say, oh I see that we had to take all those turns to get here.

The story starts with another death, that of Sam's sister, my Aunt Leah. When she died several years ago, it was not unexpected; she'd been sick for a long time. I found her shrunken and

1. "Under African Skies," Paul Simon.

tiny in the hospital bed, in the nursing home where she spent her last days. But she was still herself, still quoting Swinburne. Only her body had shriveled. She acknowledged me in her usual cursory fashion, and then immediately focused on more important concerns: the utter stupidity of George Bush—here she let loose a blast of curses I'd never heard from her before, except when she'd been drinking—but, she was sad to say, that since she couldn't really do him in like she wanted to, she decided she was ready to go herself and be done with the whole goddamn thing. But there was something she wanted to tell me first.

"Come closer," she whispered hoarsely, her claw-like fingers stretching towards me. "I want to make sure you understand me."

"I'm ready to go," she said. "Because I saw them, they're waiting for me."

I wasn't sure who they were. I didn't know what, if anything, she believed about an afterlife; she'd never been a particularly religious Jew or a spiritual anything as far as I knew. But I didn't want to appear as ignorant as I felt, so I murmured what I hoped was an appropriately solemn, response and waited.

"Elma was there," she whispered. "And Sam, too." (Sam dead these 67 years, buried in an unmarked grave in Spain. The beloved oldest son, the one they never got over losing.) "They're waiting for me."

She sounded so small, so trusting and reassured, so unlike her acerbic, cynical self, that I didn't want to break the magical moment. But I needed to ask. When else would I have the opportunity?

"What did he look like?" a question I hadn't intended, but what flew out of my mouth next was even more spontaneous. "Did he look like he did when you last saw him? Or was he an old man?"

Scowling, she cracked open one eye, squinting up at me, her expression letting me know that this was just about the stupidest question she'd ever been asked: "Young, of course. Handsome. Strong. Not big, but strong. Just like the day he left for Spain."

"He smiled at me," she murmured, drifting away.

I had been dismissed and I took my leave then. Leah took hers a couple of days later.

She didn't want to be buried. Her tiny body was donated to "medical science," a corpse for medical students to pore over and dissect. Not one of them would ever know that she could quote the entire Rime of the Ancient Mariner by heart.

Years before, during happier days, Leah had asked me, if, when it was time, I would scatter her ashes. She was standing on my porch, pointing towards the river. "There. That'd be a good place. I always did love the water."

I promised, hoping that the day I'd have to fulfill my promise was years away.

Even after she died I didn't give my promise much thought. Don't medical students work on their cadaver for a year?

But, just three months later, the morning of my son's seventeenth birthday, there was a knock at the door. I was on the phone, engrossed in planning a surprise party for him. My daughter, Hannah, and I had secretly invited the entire debate team, ordered fifteen pizzas, and were in the throes of trying to figure out how to get the guests there without Josh catching wind of it. I didn't want to be distracted from the task at hand, so I waited a minute hoping that whoever knocked would go away.

But I didn't wait quite long enough, because a UPS truck was just pulling out of the driveway when I stuck my head out the door. The uniformed driver saw me, and jumped out of his truck holding a small package.

"Are you Laurie Levinger?" Yes, I was. "I have this package for you. Can you sign for it please?"

I barely looked at what I was signing for, I just signed, and went back inside holding whatever it was.

There was no return address. I tore the brown paper off. The small ordinary-looking cardboard box had a label. Golden Glow Crematorium.

Leah had arrived.

But I didn't greet her properly. I couldn't deal with her. I had a party to give.

The dead would have to wait.

Leah sat in her box in the garage until the winter thaw; a perfect time to celebrate water. I hiked to the spot she had pointed out, and scattered her ashes from a spit of land that jutted into the river. But what appeared to be solid ground was in reality half-frozen muck, which sucked me in. As I stood there, knee-deep in icy reeds, I reached into the box and withdrew a pinch of ashes, tossing them lightly away. I said the Kaddish, scattered most of the ashes, and waded back to shore. A gentle breeze blew ashes off the water towards me.

I saved a tiny portion. I figured that later, if I was ever ready, if I ever needed her, Leah could accompany me to Spain.

Spain. Sam—adventurer, idealist, boy-hero—was buried there in that unmarked grave. No one had ever made the trip to visit him.

It seemed unlikely, grandiose maybe, to think that I could bring Leah to him. Because I didn't know where he was in Spain.

How in the world would I find him?

23

Searching for Sam

LAURIE

THIS CHAPTER includes details of the circuitous route that led me to Sam, and provides the answer to the question I have been asked many times: How did you find him?

Once I learned that Leah believed Sam was waiting for her, after I'd read Sam's letters and Elma's unpublished novels, *Death in the Mountains* and *New Hills and Towers*, I decided to try again to ask my father questions, the answers to which might help fill in the blanks. But he had little to say, our conversation punctuated by long silences. Finally after one of these awkward pauses, we made an unspoken agreement and transitioned to discussing the political climate of the 1930s. Here he was knowledgeable and eloquent.

Stymied in the attempt to get personal information from the sole survivor that I knew from the period, I turned to books. I focused initially on first-person accounts of veterans of the Abraham Lincoln Brigade, and then read more academic texts. I also began research on the Internet, and this turned up the first tenuous lead to Sam.

When they were in high school my children, Josh and Hannah, had been captivated by the *idea* of Sam Levinger, the idealistic young man who died "fighting the good fight". Each of them did their sophomore year project about Sam. Josh wrote an award-winning research paper; Hannah won a recitation contest performing Sam's farewell letter.

Later, Josh posted his research paper on the Internet. Later still, a rabbi named Mark Samuel Hurvitz read the paper; he contacted Josh explaining that he recognized the Levinger name, because his father had been a student of Sam's father, Rabbi Lee Levinger, at Ohio State University. And, in fact, Mark added, his middle name is Samuel. For Samuel Levinger.

A year or so later a man named Dale Belman contacted Rabbi Mark Hurvitz asking him for information about progressive movements at OSU during the 1930s. Rabbi Hurvitz referred Dale Belman to Josh's webpage.

Although I knew all of this, I didn't think about Rabbi Hurvitz or Dale Belman until I began searching for Sam. I emailed Dale Belman, describing the project. Dale Belman, it turned out, is the son of Clara Belman (*neé* Distel), Sam's girlfriend at Ohio State. Within a couple of hours Dale wrote back saying that he had a box of his mother's papers that included letters from Sam when he was in Spain. Did I want him to send them to me?

While I waited to receive Clara Distel's papers, I continued my research at the Abraham Lincoln Brigade Archives website. Biographical data has been collected for most of the volunteers. The information about Sam was that he had been wounded at the battle of Belchite and died in a hospital at La Puebla de Hijar. This stands in direct contradiction to eyewitness accounts and descriptions of his death on the battlefield.

So where did Sam die? And when? And where was he buried?

Continuing to follow the thread, I spoke to a friend, a "red diaper baby" who referred me to Dr. Tony Geist, a professor at the University of Washington who had made a film about the Brigade, (*Souls Without Borders, 1936–2006: The Untold Story of the Abraham Lincoln Brigade*) and to Peter Carroll, author of *The Odyssey of the Abraham Lincoln Brigade*.

Dr. Geist gave me the address of Jeanne Houck, director of Abraham Lincoln Brigade Archives in New York. She then referred me to Gail Malmgreen, the archivist at the Tainiment Library at New York University.

Ms. Houke also referred me to Alan Warren, an Englishman who lives in Spain and gives tours of Spanish Civil War battle-grounds. I wrote Mr. Warren describing the search for Sam's grave, and asking if he had any information about Sam's life and death in Spain. He offered to help with research in Spain.

In June 2010 Josh and I went to New York City to meet with Gail Malmgreen and Jeanne Houke at the Abraham Lincoln Brigade Archive. Sam's file was almost empty, except for a group photo of a machine gun unit. I had this same photo at home, but had not been able to identify any of the men. This photograph was labeled "the Tom Mooney Company", and Sam's name was written on the back. Ms. Malmgreen located the ship's manifest of the *S.S. Paris*, which sailed on January 16, 1937. Sam's name was on the list (along with one hundred other volunteers, including Dr. Edward Barsky).

Alan Warren wrote that, in spite of the information in the Archive, he believed it was most likely that Sam was killed in the Battle of Belchite. He referred me to several books in which Sam's death on the battlefield is described. But he offered to get in touch with a local person doing research about the field hospital that had been at La Puebla de Hijar (a mobile hospital which no longer exists). And he sent me *White Sheets,* Steve Nelson's gripping de-scription of being treated at that hospital.

Hannah and I went to the Brandeis University Library where they have an extensive collection about the Spanish Civil War. The librarian gave us access to original photos from the Charles Korbin collection and original scrapbooks in which we found the announcement of Sam's death in *The Citizen*, the Columbus, Ohio newspaper.

I received the box from Dale Belman. Included were Sam's letters to Clara as well as the letter that Rueben Ryant wrote to Sam's parents after his death. He states that Sam was "cut down" at Belchite.

It is unclear from Rueben's eyewitness account whether Sam was wounded or killed on the battlefield.

However, Alan Warren's research in Spain uncovered irrefutable evidence that Sam died on September 5, 1937 at the field hospital at La Puebla de Hijar. He sent me a copy of the original death certificate.

Now we knew where Sam was wounded and where he died. But where was he buried?

It might be a good thing to go to Spain.

24

December 2010

Salud

LAURIE

ARAGON: THE terrain is rough and forbidding. Winter-dry, barren, desolate. And cold. I'd read that it was brutally cold the winter of 1937. Living in the open trenches at Jarama and Brunete, many of the men got frostbite. At Brunete, Sam was wounded a second time and his commanding officer, Hans Amlie, ordered him to return home to the States to do political work. He wrote Elma, asking if she thought he should come home, or stay on as a truck driver.

We stopped first at the train station at La Puebla de Hijar, where we'd been told that Sam would've disembarked for his final battle. But I knew from one of his stories that this isn't the route he took. In reality, he deserted from the hospital in Madrid and hitch-hiked for four days—that's when he wrote Elma all about green grapes and figs—to rejoin his machine gun company. Of course, he didn't mention that he'd left the hospital against orders.

Sam found his battalion on the outskirts of Belchite, holed up in an olive grove. The medieval town was surrounded by walls; there are two churches standing sentinel on the edges of the town each with a bell tower perfect for snipers. The fascists always occupied the church bell towers, the highest place in any town. Sam's company had already laid siege, a siege that would go on for days before Franco's forces finally surrendered on September 6th.

Sam and his comrades knew that Belchite must be taken, for strategic reasons and reasons of morale. Impenetrable Belchite, the town that had defeated Napoleon in another war. Now fascist forces were keeping the town's residents captive. The Republicans must take Belchite. But at what cost?

The walled medieval town Sam saw bears little resemblance to the Belchite we walk through today. Rubble-strewn, piles of broken rock where streets had been. Gaping holes in roofs that had protected families from rain, blazing sun, wind and snow.

Remnants. Silent brooding skeletons of San Augustin and San Martin, those two churches where families had prayed, babies had been baptized, young men and women had gotten married, and the dead had been mourned.

Remnants of glorious carvings of saints and lambs, and frescoed walls that have—somehow—survived the ravages of bombs, weather and time. Echoes of another life.

I had thought the land desolate until we walked the streets of Belchite, with only ghosts for company. Phantoms: praying, strolling home from church for Sunday dinner, sitting around a table in a second floor apartment with the clear blue walls. Colors of the Aragon sky. After coffee, leaning over balconies to gossip with neighbors on the street below.

Silent Belchite.

Murdered Belchite.

Ghost residents plead, "Remember us. Remember."

Later we drove back to La Puebla de Hijar. Even today on good roads it's a long drive. What had it been like for Sam seventy-three years ago in an ambulance, praying that the bombs would not find him?

In the town cemetery we found a small stone memorial for the Republican dead. The men who died in the field hospital were buried here in a mass grave.

We had found Sam. We chanted the Kaddish, the Jewish prayer for the dead. The ancient Aramaic words were not a comfort to the dead, but they brought us full circle. *Yis-ga-dal v-ys-ka-dash sh-mai-rabbo . . .*

We each placed a stone on the memorial. I said: Uncle Sam. I wish I'd known you. You gave us a model of courage, fighting for what you believe in, making a commitment and putting your body on the line. You lived your ideals and your passions. Your younger brother, my father, lived his life from that place, too, and, because of his example; we have that to always strive for. Staughton Lynd, and how many others? became activists because of you and your comrades. You left a legacy and a written record behind. Which is how we've gotten to know you. You would have been one of the great writers of your generation. We remember you. We salute you.

I scattered Leah's ashes. Sister and brother together, outside of time.

And we left a small granite marker with Sam's dates and the revolutionary greeting. *Salud.*

ELMA

And there are two worlds—the world we live in and the world we cannot see. If we could bridge that gap—but we cannot. Yet sometimes the veil between the worlds is so very thin. You walk beside me and in every weakness I lean upon your arm—so hard, so strong, so young. I gave that I have—and now nothing can take you from me.

> When he came in, he always called Mother, are you there?
> Sometimes still I still pretend
> I hear him.
> And I answer, yes, son I'm here.[1]

1. Private collection.

Afterword

LAURIE

O N THE way to Belchite we stayed overnight in Fuendetodos, a medieval village where eighty hardy residents live during the winter. In the summer, tourists flock to the village to visit the home of Goya and a small museum dedicated to his work.

Esther Bosque, the proprietor of the two hundred-year-old house where we stayed, asked what we were doing in Fuendetodos in the middle of the winter. When I explained about trying to find where Sam was buried, her expression changed from polite inquiry to deep sadness.

"My grandparents were with the Republicans," she said. "They were poor farmers. War is a terrible, terrible thing."

"I would like to hear what happened to your family," I said. "If you would like to tell me the story."

"Oh, yes." Esther put her arm around me. "Thank you for what your family did for our people."

ESTHER

My grandparents were farmers, poor ones, with just a few bits of land to work and four children: Araceli (12 years old when the Spanish Civil War broke out), Ambrosio (9 years old), Antonio (my father, 7 years old), and Maribel (4). They lived in a simple house, with two horse to work the land.

My grandfather belonged to the CNT (National Workers' Confederation) and was a Republican sympathizer, along with his brother, Miguel. They lived in Mezalocha (Zaragosa), a small vil-

153

lage near Fuendetodos, but "the Nationalists," Franco's army, was in Mezalocha.

One night, they came looking for them and locked them in jail. Early the next day they took them to the mountain with other men from nearby villages, made them dig graves and put them up against the wall. They shot the other men from the other villages but not the two of them, they didn't shoot them.

They took them back to the jail and when the guards weren't looking, my grandfather escaped, but his brother Miguel was convinced that they weren't going to kill them and didn't want to abandon his children.

My grandfather Felix said goodbye to his family, took the horses, and went to work the land, but he abandoned his horses (which went home alone) and set out walking through the mountains to Barcelona. He took shelter in a relative's house until he left for a refugee camp in France, but another relative in France helped him get out.

As for his brother Miguel, they came looking for him that same morning and this time they shot him, without any trial or explanation.

After a few days, since my grandfather didn't show up they came looking for my grandmother and arrested her, they shaved her head and hit her, but she couldn't say where my grandfather was, since she didn't even know where he was hiding or what had happened to him. She was held for 4 or 5 months, and when she came home, where she had left four children in the care of her brother and parents, she was sick, in pain, and died a few months later. They never saw each other again, since my grandfather couldn't come back.

My grandfather spent World War II in France, working on a farm. He didn't come back until 10 years later. My grandparents never saw each other again, ever.

My father and his brothers lived off the charity of his aunt. Ambrosio (nine years old), and my father at seven worked their parents' land. Their older sister had to wash other people's clothes and take care of her brothers. Their younger sister never got over being orphaned and has always been in psychiatric treatment, living a more or less normal life but always with medical concerns.

This is the story of my grandparents, but there were thousands more like it, or worse."[1]

THE END

1. private correspondence with author, 2011.

Appendix

In case of death only, please send this to
Mrs. Lee J. Levinger, 2257 Indianola Ave.
Columbus, Ohio, U. S. A.
Do not send in case of injury.
Thanks, comrade.

Samuel Levinger

Dear Mother and Father:

I suppose that by the time you receive this, I will have been dead
several weeks. Of course, war is a confused thing, and I have seen
enough certified corpses walking around to make me a little skep-
tical, but if you receive this and an official announcement too,
count it as definite.

This is the last day of relief. We are going up to some front tomorrow to clear out the Fascists. I do not doubt that we will be
successful in repatriating the boys across the street, but it will be
at considerable cost, and as the Lincoln Battalion is good it should
be in the middle of it.

I still stick by my original conviction that I will be alive long after
a whole lot of dictators have died of lead poisoning or hardened
arteries; but I've been wrong on other matters before. Hence I decided to write this letter.

Certainly I am not enthusiastic about dying. I've gotten a good bit of fun out of my first twenty years despite the fact that, except for the last six months they were pretty useless. I suppose I would have enjoyed my next twenty just as much. I wanted to write this letter, however, to make clear that there is absolutely nothing to regret.

If I were alive again I think I would join in the battle again at this crucial place. There was an extremely important job to do over here and I was one of the men who decided to do it. That a good many of us were killed while doing it is unfortunate, and the fact that I was killed is still more unfortunate from our standpoints. However, this has no relevance to the necessity of doing the job. This difference between world Fascist and world socialism is too great to permit out safeties to be a factor for consideration.

Next I want to beg both of you not to see this out of context. World change is a stern master. It had killed and will kill millions of boys as dear to somebody as I am to you. The Fascists want war, and bitter war we will give them.

You are more fortunate than many of the parents, for you still have two children with extremely bright futures. You have your extremely valuable work. I am less able to evaluate Father's work, though I realize its great worth; but in my field, that of an author, I can say I think Mother should become one of the most valuable authors of the generation. And you still have the emancipation of America to be achieved.

I think my ideas on immortality agree largely with yours. I once wrote a lousy poem "If there is darkness beyond I shall sleep, if light I shall wake." So if I meet you folks again all to the good—if not, we've had quite a bit of pleasure in each other's company while it lasted.

As for my friends, give them my love if you run across them. Tell them I said there's only one thing to remember—that there's one comrade less to do the job of soldier of discontent. They'll all have to do some work to make up for my getting perforated. See if that will get a few of these mugwumps into action.

This has been a clumsy letter. I just want to say that I love you both a great deal, and so forth. Also that it isn't such a serious thing.

Love and revolutionary greetings.
Joy to the world.

Samuel Levinger

Bibliography

Acier, Marcel, ed. *From Spanish Trenches: Recent Letters from Spain*. New York: Modern Age, 1937.

Barsky, Edward K., and Elizabeth Waugh. "The Surgeon Goes to War." Unpublished manuscript.

Bessie, Alvah. *Alvah Bessie's Spanish Civil War Notebooks*. Edited by Dan Bessie. Lexington: The University Press of Kentucky, 2002.

———, ed. *The Heart of Spain: Anthology of Fiction, Non-fiction, and Poetry*. New York: Veterans of the Abraham Lincoln Brigade, 1952.

———. *Men in Battle: A Story of Americans in Spain*. New York: Veterans of the Abraham Lincoln Brigade, 1954.

Camus, Albert, et. al. *L'Espagne Libre*. Paris: Calmann-Levy, 1945.

Capa, Robert. *Death in the Making*. New York: Covici-Friede, 1938.

———, et. al. *Heart of Spain: Robert Capa's Photographs of the Spanish Civil War*. Hong Kong: Aperture, 2005.

Carroll, Peter N. *The Odyssey of the Abraham Lincoln Brigade: Americans in the Spanish Civil War*. Stanford: Stanford University Press, 1994.

De La Mora, Constancia. *In Place of Splendor: The Autobiography of a Spanish Woman*. New York: Harcourt, 1939.

Eby, Cecil. *Between the Bullet and the Lie: American Volunteers in the Spanish Civil War*. New York: Holt, Reinhart and Winston, 1969.

———. *Comrades and Commissars: The Lincoln Battalion in the Spanish Civil War*. University Park: The Pennsylvania State University Press, 2007.

Faber, Sebastiaan, and James D. Fernandez. "The War Before the Lights Went Out: An Interview with Helen Graham." *The Volunteer*, March 2010.

Fisher, Harry. *Comrades: Tales of a Brigadista in the Spanish Civil War*. Lincoln: University of Nebraska Press, 1997.

Graham, Helen. *The Spanish Civil War: A Very Short Introduction*. New York: Oxford University Press, 2005.

Hemingway, Ernest. *For Whom the Bell Tolls*. New York: Scribner, 1940.

Katz, William Loren, and Marc Crawford. *The Lincoln Brigade: A Picture History*. New York: Atheneum, 1989.

Kempton, Murray. *Part Of Our Time: Some Ruins and Monuments of the Thirties*. New York: New York Review Books, 1998.

Landis, Arthur H. *Death in the Olive Groves: American Volunteers in the Spanish Civil War 1936-1939*. New York: Paragon House, 1989.

Lee, Laurie. *A Moment of War: A Memoir of the Spanish Civil War*. New York: The New Press, 1991.

Levinger, Elma. "Death in the Mountains." Unpublished manuscript, 1940.

———. "New Hills and Towers." Unpublished manuscript, 1946.

Levinger, Joseph. Personal interview with author, 2010.

Levinger, Leah. Unpublished oral history, 1950 and 1974.

Levinger, Lee. *A Jewish Chaplain in France*. New York: Macmillan, 1921.

———. "The Volunteer for Liberty." Veterans of the International Brigades (American Chapter), 1938.

Levinger, Samuel. Unpublished poems and stories, 1937.

——— [R. P., pseud.]. "With the International Brigade," *The Nation*, May 8, 1937.

Lynd, Staughton. "Labor History, Oral History, and May 4." Friends of the Kent State University Libraries. April 15, 1998.

Merriman, Marion, and Warren Lerude. *American Commander in Spain: Robert Hale Merriman and the Abraham Lincoln Brigade*. Reno: University of Nevada Press, 1986.

Nelson, Cary, and Jefferson Hendricks. *Madrid 1937: Letters of the Abraham Lincoln Brigade From the Spanish Civil War*. New York: Routledge, 1996.

Nelson, Steve. *The Volunteers: A Personal Narrative of the Fight Against Fascism in Spain*. New York: Masses and Mainstream, 1953.

Neruda, Pablo. *Memoirs*. New York: Farrar, Straus and Giroux, 1974.

———. *Spain in Our Hearts*. New York: New Directions, 2005.

Neugass, James. *War Is Beautiful: An American Ambulance Driver in the Spanish Civil War*. New York: The New Press, 2008.

Osheroff, Abe, and Bill Susman. *No Pasarán! The 50th Anniversary Of the Lincoln Brigade*. New York: The Abraham Lincoln Brigade Archives, 1986.

Orwell, George. *Homage To Catalonia*. New York: Harcourt Brace, 1952.

———. *Collected Essays*. London. Mercury, 1961.

Plenn, Abel. *Wind in the Olive Trees: Spain from Inside*. New York: Book Find Club, 1946.

Ripps, A. *The Story of the Abraham Lincoln Battalion, Written in the Trenches of Spain*. New York: Friends of the Abraham Lincoln Battalion, 1937.

Rosenstone, Robert A. *Crusade of the Left: The Lincoln Battalion in the Spanish Civil War*. New York: Pegasus, 1969.

Seldes, George. *Witness to a Century: Encounters with the Noted, the Notorious, and the Three SOBs*. New York: Ballantine, 1987.

Sperber, Murray A. *And I Remember Spain: A Spanish Civil War Anthology.* New York: Macmillan, 1974.

Tremlett, Giles. *Ghosts of Spain: Travels Through Spain And Its Silent Past.* New York: Walker, 2006.

Wolff, Milton. *Another Hill: An Autobiographical Novel.* Chicago: University of Illinois Press, 1994.